Understanding Behaviour and Development in Early Childhood

In this accessible and thought-provoking text, the author examines the behaviour of babies and young children in a developmental context, and takes into account the shifts and changes over time as young children grow and mature.

Understanding Behaviour and Development in Early Childhood reveals, for example, how behaviour perceived as 'difficult' in a young child may be the manifestation of a response to emotional, sensory and cognitive experiences. Throughout the book readers will find a strong emphasis on emotional well-being and the need to place our understanding of behaviour within a developmental timeframe.

Based on wide-ranging professional experience, the topics examined and discussed in this insightful book include:

- what we understand by 'behaviour'
- how the brain and senses work and mature during early childhood
- behaviour as a reflection of the child's internal state
- what emotions are and how we learn what feelings mean to us as individuals
- how emotions affect our ability to learn
- how we develop a sense of self.

The book provides suggestions for how adults may think about and respond to changes in children's behaviour, and how we may support children in learning how to manage their own behaviour as they grow older and encounter wider and more complex situations.

Understanding the meaning of behaviour is a constant challenge for anyone working with children. This developmental approach promotes a helpful reflective stance for practitioners and students working in early childhood education and care.

Maria Robinson was a health visitor and counsellor and currently is a lecturer, trainer and independent adviser in early years development. Her doctorate is in child welfare and protection.

Understanding Behaviour and Development in Early Childhood

A guide to theory and practice

Maria Robinson

 Routledge
Taylor & Francis Group

LONDON AND NEW YORK

KH

First edition published 2011
by Routledge
2 Park Square, Milton Park, Abingdon, Oxon, OX14 4RN

Simultaneously published in the USA and Canada
by Routledge
270 Madison Avenue, New York, NY 10016

Routledge is an imprint of the Taylor & Francis Group, an informa business

© 2011 Maria Robinson

Typeset in Garamond and GillSans by
Swales & Willis Ltd, Exeter, Devon
Printed and bound in Great Britain by
CPI Antony Rowe, Chippenham, Wiltshire

British Library Cataloguing in Publication Data
A catalogue record for this book is available
from the British Library

Library of Congress Cataloging-in-Publication Data
Robinson, Maria.
  Understanding behaviour and development in early childhood: a
  guide to theory and practice / Maria Robinson.
   p. cm.
  Includes bibliographical references.
  1. Behavior modification. 2. Early childhood education.
  3. Classroom management. I. Title.
  LB1060.2.R625 2011
  305.231—dc22   2010011560

ISBN13: 978-0-415-56560-8 (hbk)
ISBN13: 978-0-415-56561-5 (pbk)
ISBN13: 978-0-203-84288-1 (ebk)

3/19/10

Contents

Preface   vii

1 Introduction   1

Managing behaviour 3
Sophisticated mammals 3
Behaving nicely 4
Where next? 6

2 A journey through the brain and the senses   8

Part 1: The brain 8
Part 2: Experiencing the world and getting to know the self 24
The importance of touch 27
Vision 29
Hearing and communication 31
Smell and taste 33
The essential nature of movement 34
Summary 37

3 Interactions, relationships and emotional responses   38

In the beginning 39
The song of the mother (and father too) 40
Lack of communication 42
Food for thought 44
The voice of the baby – the separation call 45
The importance of faces 46
Food for thought 49
Imitating me, imitating you 50
The story continues 53
Attachment security – a defence against danger 54

4   **Time-related emergence of skills and abilities, growth and change**   56

Tick tock – the relentless ticking of the developmental clock 57
A glance back 58
A widening world – towards the child's first birthday 59
Entering the second year and towards preschool 67
Joy, tears, temper tantrums and 'little Neros' 70
Temper tantrums – those storms 71
Little Neros 71
Moving out of the storm 74
Flights of fancy 74
I'm so afraid – the emergence of fears and phobias, and aggression 76
Summary 77

5   **The adult: awareness, sensitivity, interpretation and responses**   78

Do what I do 81
Attachment needs 82
Separations and settling 84
Loss and grief 85
Something strange where danger lurks 87
Interpreting behaviour 89
Looking through the gender lens – expectations and interpretations 91
The environment 94
Summary 97

6   **Behaviour as the self's mirror**   98

What is a child? A wider view 99
Back to the child and behaviour 105
What kind of society do we want? 106

Notes   107
Bibliography   111
Index   119

Preface

The child as person – behaviour as communication

The aim of this book is to support those working with children and their families to better understand a child's behaviour. It is suggested that the fundamental foundations of a child's behaviour lie in overlapping frameworks comprising:

- brain growth and maturation
- the impact of sensory information
- the quality of interactions and relationships
- the broadly time related emergence of skills and abilities, growth and change
- the impact of the adult's own 'internal world', their perceptions, attitudes, expectations and interpretations of the child's behavioural cues.

All these form part of a jigsaw – each piece contributing to the types of behaviour we may encounter and/or witness in a child and our responses which further influence outcomes.

Thinking of behaviour within the context of these frameworks allows for reflection both on their specific influence and their *combined* effect. Reflection on how the brain appears to function and mature together with the role of the senses provides information as to how the child may perceive and organize their experiences. The impact of the quality of early relationships, how adults react to the child's needs and their emotional impact links with both brain and sensory development. This is then entwined with the ongoing, broadly time-related unfolding of skills and abilities. It will be suggested that the stage or phase of the child's development may link strongly with the types of behaviour seen in most children during such phases. For example, the strivings for independence in the toddler may lead to more defiant or negative behaviour than might have previously been experienced by the parent. Another example is the emergence of the concept of object permanence and how this may influence the child's withdrawal or approach strategies to unfamiliar people. However, as well as behaviour which may reflect a shift in the child's abilities, there are also those actions which are part of simply being a human child growing up, such as exploratory behaviour, the expression of emotions and the need for play. The final framework links to the adult role, perspectives and expectations and how these can impact on the way in which behaviour can be interpreted.

Such frameworks allow for consideration that behaviour is an outward expression of the child's internal world at any particular phase, influenced by both past experience and immediate context. In other words, how children react and interact both to their experiences and those around them will reflect a moment-by-moment state of feeling in the present embedded in the child's emotional history – behaviour *is* communication.

Adults must always try to view the child with compassion, remember their role as guide and mentor and that children nearly always require adults to be stronger, wiser and fundamentally in charge. In the end, therefore, this book aims to support you in bringing both heart and mind to bear on the needs of the child.

Chapter 1

Introduction

A while ago, while sitting at breakfast, my husband was thinking over an invitation by a friend to go away for a few days. He was debating times, travel and so on and all the while I was conscious of a tight, unpleasant feeling in my stomach accompanied by a subtle sense of dread. Outwardly I was aware of speaking reasonably sensibly while at the same time aware that these feelings were growing into a sensation of panic. Later, reflecting on my inward reactions to this simple, non-threatening situation, I tried to make sense of it. True, I didn't like being on my own at night (in spite of the comforting presence of two dogs!), nor did I resent or dislike the idea of my husband being away with a friend – in fact, I felt he deserved a break. So, what was the source of this sense of anxiety and panic? With a sigh of insight, I realized that the reaction was the faint echo of the pain and fear of abandonment – unfortunately a rather too common feature of my very early years. However, these uncomfortable feelings did not overwhelm my responses in this particular situation – in other words, I was able to cope with them and use my awareness that they were out of kilter to the situation, and so modify my reactions. Had I not, I could have had a range of responses to my husband, some of which may have been very unhelpful! In other words, my behaviour could have been a direct reflection of my feelings, raw and unmodified with only a limited view of possible options.

Without reflection and an ability to cope and consequently *behave* in a way that reflected the *actual* situation rather than the ancient echoes of old fears, my actions could have resembled those of the emotionally hurt and frightened child, fearful of being left. Not only children, but teenagers and adults who have not had support and help in being able to cope with their feelings may simply react as if they were threatened or in danger – sometimes in ways totally out of proportion to the particular circumstance. An example is that at the time of writing (2009) a dreadful incident is in the news of a woman who had bleach thrown at her because she told some young people to be quiet in a cinema: a non-threatening situation responded to in a way that of itself was appalling but also completely out of any relevance or correspondence to the original situation.

I have told you about this simple example from daily life and a news item because they highlight some of the ideas/concepts which will be discussed later in this book, The core argument will be that adult responses to our earliest awareness of threat/

danger and subsequent distress provide the first and most powerful template for our subsequent behaviour. First, as I am sure most readers will be aware, feelings evoked in our earliest years are very powerful and their footprint on our individual psychological development may influence responses from childhood through the lifespan. Second, the imprint of those feelings can arise in the most innocent of circumstances, as demonstrated above. However because they contain *elements* of the original situations – they can trigger corresponding physiological and emotional reactions. Third, our ability to manage our feelings and adjust our behaviour changes as we get older. These changes are both in the *manner* that we deal with them and in our levels of *understanding* of why we feel and act as we do. Therefore this book considers the influences that help us cope. It also has to be recognized that along with changes in our levels of being able to think about our feelings, we need to have the *opportunities* to do so. When working for a while in a hospice, I was so sad to note that for many of the patients their terminal illness was the 'wake up' call for them to rethink relationships and to reflect on how they had lived their life. Indeed, I imagine that for many of us it is often a crisis that provides a time for reassessing how we might be reacting and responding to others and whether we want to change the way we feel and behave and perhaps seeking help in which to do so.

I have talked about the central core to this book and indeed the hypothesis presented is that much of the behaviour we observe in children is also a reflection of their inner world and all its accompanying sensations. A very interesting quote from Goethe, the world-famous German novelist, reads: 'Behaviour is the mirror in which everyone shows their image.' As babies and very young children, how we behave is, perhaps more than at any other time in our lives, an image of the *feeling* self – not yet overlain by understanding of social expectations and learning how we may need to hide how we feel dependent on context. The baby and very young child simply *is*.

At this time in our lives, our very powerful emotions are accompanied by only a very, very limited capacity to cope with them because of the immaturity of those areas in the brain that coordinate feelings and responses. Obviously, too, babies and very young children are also extremely limited in being able to react physically to a situation both in asking for help or seeking reassurance. Their means of communication are powerful through crying or seeking behaviour, but this relies on the sensitive interpretation of their needs by adults. Therefore the vital role of parents and other carers involved in the day-to-day life of a child is the responsibility of helping, supporting and meeting the needs of the child through their understanding of what the child is trying to express. In order to do this, for parents and everyone involved in the lives of children, we require a degree of self-awareness and understanding of our emotional responses to the child and the context. This will allow us to appreciate that sometimes our responses and reactions based on our individual life experiences will influence how competent we feel to support the child. We need to have awareness of our particular strengths and emotionally tender places when dealing with the many complexities of such involvement.

Managing behaviour

One of the concerns that can arise when thinking about the behaviour of young children is that there may be a tendency to focus on how we adults *manage* their behaviour, together with advice on the strategies available to support this management from 'naughty steps' to reward stickers and so on. I don't want to demean these strategies in any way as adults can find them helpful in many circumstances. However, the emphasis in this book is not about strategies nor will it tell you what you might do in different circumstances. What this book does aim to do is to support thinking about what lies *behind* behaviour – what is the 'heart of the intended communication', the lovely phrase from the therapist Mary Sue Moore.[1] In other words, what is the child trying to tell us about their current state of feeling when they behave in a particular way? Such a stance has a mirror in the best types of care given to those with dementia, and there are significant parallels between what someone may need at a time in their life when their understanding is becoming increasingly limited and the needs of children. Each end of the spectrum of life requires that carers – in whatever context – need to recognize the individual as a person first. Elinor Goldschmied in her seminal work regarding play and day care practice referred to '*People* under 3', and in this work too it is this concept of the child as a person which will be at the heart of this communication from me to you.

Sophisticated mammals

We humans are certainly wonderful and complex beings, but in many ways so are other creatures. For example, the capacity to communicate in often very sophisticated ways is present in a range of other species, such as the 'waggle dance' of the honey bee alerting other forager bees to the location of pollen. This complex 'figure of eight' dance provides accurate spatial information on direction and distance. Communication in sound by creatures such as bats, dolphins and elephants is well known but not really fully understood. The uniqueness of our capacity for verbal communication perhaps does not lie in our ability to make sounds with meaning but rather what we are able to *do* with those words, and that they can represent thoughts, ideas, plans and dreams as well as feelings not only vocally but represented in sign as well. Once children acquire language in either medium they have a tool that allows them to label, categorize and organize the environment that they have only sensed and experienced until that point. We are able to use communication to encompass abstractions such as past and future as well as the present. Children's behaviour is supported by language as they are (one hopes) increasingly provided with labels for their feelings as well as those concepts that they are acquiring, such as large, small, next to, beside, in front of and so on; categories such as dog, cat, ball; properties such as round, soft, hard, heavy; and relationships such as mum, dad, granny, friend.

While there are certainly differences in the levels of abstraction, capacity for thought and expressiveness, tool use and creativity between ourselves and our closest relatives – the primates – there are also differences between mammals in general and other species. This is probably down to differences in 'higher' brain structures (see Chapter 2). There are also many commonalities which are shared, such as mating, protection of young, pair bonds, separation, loss and survival in the face of danger. A particular trait we have in common with other species is that we live in social groups. While individuals may choose or be forced to live in relative isolation, mostly we live alongside and with other humans. Within these groups, large and small, there develops commonly accepted ways of behaviour and as Dugatkin (2002a) says, while brain size may affect a culture's complexity, even creatures with very tiny brains offer 'extraordinary examples of culture and its interaction with genetics' (p.51).

The particular way in which Dugatkin uses the word 'culture' is in the context of the process of 'cultural transmission'. We learn how to do things by observing others – imitating them – including, of course, watching how others behave in particular situations. Observations of chimps, both in the wild and in sanctuary environments, have demonstrated that while they may share a common genetic template with one another, their social/cultural behaviour can vary widely dependent on the context in which they live. For example, chimps can learn new behaviours that spread throughout a local chimp population, and Dugatkin notes sixty-five behaviours that are 'cultural variants' have been identified among different populations. This adaptability and diversity is certainly true of humans. We all share the same human species DNA, with our various individual traits influenced by the particular variations from our own parents and their history. However, while how we are raised in our family will fine-tune our particular personalities and responses, we will also be influenced by the broader environment and social/cultural context in which we live. In every culture, there may be subtle differences in the way emotions are allowed to be expressed or which behaviours are seen as acceptable or not.[2]

It seems to me that in order to understand the behaviour of children (and ourselves) we should not dismiss the findings from research on other species. As well as the cultural transmission of 'how we might do things' from guppies to chimps, the behaviour of many primates and other sophisticated mammals such as elephants, including the types of play engaged in by their young and responses to nurture, loss and grief, provide a mirror – if we are prepared to look – at the sorts of reactions and responses that we see in very young children. Elephants, for example, show behaviours that reflect the trauma they have suffered. A very interesting source is the David Sheldrick Wildlife Trust[3] and the rescue work they do with orphaned elephants, rhino and other animals. The intensive care these troubled animals need, the close relationships they make with their keepers and the prolonged periods of time some need in order to learn to trust bears a strong relationship with the way in which troubled young children will seek comfort or display difficult behaviours in response to their experiences. As the well-known playworker and teacher Bob Hughes (2001) says, 'we are a species amongst other species'.

Behaving nicely

When parents and other professionals talk about behaviour, what we are alluding to, usually, is unwanted or challenging behaviour and therefore what we can do about it – hence all those strategies! But what can be classed as desirable as well as 'unwanted' behaviour can cover a multitude of situations and contexts. To take an extreme example, stealing might be seen as an acceptable (and even desirable) behaviour if the whole family is involved in such activity. Adult attitudes towards what a child is doing is framed by what we would like the behaviour to be, and such attitudes will be governed by our individual 'moral compass', context and the social and cultural milieu which is familial as well as local and national. Children's behaviour, therefore, is framed by both individual and group adult expectations and broadly agreed social boundaries.

This leads to what perhaps is the crux when talking about behaviour in young children, which is whether our expectations are realistic and appropriate to a child's developmental stage and perhaps also to their gender. This last comment may seem a little contentious but while it is just as inappropriate to allow boys, for example, to attack one another with intent because 'boys will be boys', it is also inappropriate to see 'play fighting/rough and tumble', an activity often favoured by boys as 'aggression'. Girls too can be seen as 'better behaved' because as a gender, girls seem to mature socially earlier than boys and appear to be more ready to sit still – with boys losing out again!

What might also need to be taken into account is whether the expectations for children to *achieve* in a particular activity are realistic, for example learning to read. Wolf (2008) notes that studies by a behavioural neurologist identified areas in the brain that need to be more mature to allow us to integrate visual, verbal and auditory information rapidly – a skill necessary for reading. These areas are not fully developed until around five years of age and it is hypothesized that these areas may mature later in boys than girls. This hypothesis seems to fit findings that boys are slower to read more fluently than girls – so perhaps expecting boys to adapt easily to reading schemes at a young age may result in the type of restlessness often perceived so negatively by adults. There also appear to be some differences in the way the world is actually perceived via the senses in males and females and so sometimes reactions to different smells, sights, sounds, tastes and tactile sensations may induce not only different individual reactions but also vary between genders. For example, a room that is too hot for boys may be 'just right' for girls. We only need to remind ourselves about how we feel when too hot to think about how a pre-verbal child may express their discomfort. These sensory differences which may lead to different types of expressive behaviour are discussed more in Chapter 2.

When we talk about wanting children to 'behave', what do we actually want them to do? The question is a large one because behaviour, as we have seen, is an expression of feelings coupled with levels of understanding and awareness of intentions. As a child, in order to be seen as having positive and acceptable behaviour by adults we need to learn how to manage our emotions in the first place and thereby respond to a situation appropriately, such as smiling and saying thank you on receipt of the computer game you already have. Behaviour is truly multifaceted as it includes our ability to express ourselves socially in an appropriate way, to be motivated to persist at a difficult task instead of 'giving up' as soon as we become frustrated, to be able to inhibit our want for something so that we don't grab or take from others. It means that we are able to think something through for ourselves so that we can *choose* how to behave – a sophisticated skill which can take years. We need to be able to *feel* kindness and sympathy towards others so that we *behave* kindly towards others, or overcome dislike or fear in order to be able to share or compromise. We need to develop *values* so that these can help to shape our daily lives, and have a *positive sense of self* so that we are able to deal with the ups and downs of life without crumbling or using others as the focus for our dismay.

In order to develop sympathy with others, a sense of values, a positive sense of self, as children we need the guidance, support, care and nurture from adults who are also role models. We can no more develop from babies into children who behave appropriately most of the time in most situations within our particular context and culture without such support, than fly to the moon. It is only on such a framework that we can then develop further through adolescence – which has its own difficulties and trials – and then into adulthood, when the child eventually becomes the adult role model for future children. Behaviour is a continuum – what we lay down in infancy and early childhood affects our later behaviour. While, of course, it is possible to change, adapt and grow psychologically through the life-span, perhaps it is easier and far less painful for all if we can set aside adult needs and place the spotlight on the needs of the child and how best we can help them develop into caring, respectful people capable of love and joy and able to withstand most of the pressures of life. Behaviour is truly the mirror of who we believe ourselves to be – for good or ill.

Where next?

So, what information is hopefully going to support us in our quest to reflect on the meaning of behaviour? A logical starting point is to have a clear understanding about child development. As noted in the Foreword, the meaning of 'development' here encompasses some broad frameworks i.e. brain maturation, and the role of the senses. As outlined earlier, we are evolutionary beings, sharing many of the emotional, physiological, biological and genetic systems with other species, and how we have evolved over the millennia has its own influence on the way in which our brains have adapted and responded over time to changing circumstances. Next, the importance of interactions/relationships and especially the emotions that arise from those interactions, allied with the physiological changes that accompany them. The other frameworks for development are the significance of broadly recognized, time-related key shifts in early skills and abilities together with the types of behaviour which may accompany such shifts and the influence of adult expectations.

The following chapters will therefore address these topics, beginning in Chapter 2 with the brain and the senses. Chapter 3 will discuss the importance of interactions, including the development of a sense of self and the powerful role of emotions and influence on learning. This will also link with information from the previous chapter. Chapter 4 will consider behaviour as a strategy for communication and also how developmental shifts reflect the changing face of the child's needs – again there will be links with the preceding chapters. Chapter 5 will consider the role of adults, while Chapter

6 will provide some concluding thoughts on the potential impact of society with its changing mores regarding what is regarded as acceptable and unacceptable behaviour in a wider context.

None of us work in a vacuum and we are all subject to the various pressures of the 24-hour culture and new technology, such as the power of the Internet with the possibility of accessing a range of human activity both positive and negative. Parents and practitioners have access to a wider range of information than perhaps was ever thought possible, which may sometimes be very helpful but may also be confusing and disorientating. Children too are confronted with direct media pressures regarding desirable toys, clothes, gadgets and so on, and also have potential access to a wide range of television and internet material which may not always be appropriate and may impact overtly or covertly on their behaviour.

However, we now turn back to reflecting on the first suggested framework –the brain and the senses.

Chapter 2

A journey through the brain and the senses

This chapter deals with the first two frameworks identified in Chapter 1, i.e. the brain and the senses thereby supporting understanding of how the 'neural footprint' of the experiences encountered by a child develop and can remain so powerful throughout life. The senses are important because the information they provide forms the material from which our feelings of being 'me' emerge and how we learn of the properties of both living and inanimate objects.

The information is therefore divided into two parts. First, how our wonderful, complex and still mysterious brain appears to work. Second, particular importance that our senses play in the way we feel about ourselves. Throughout these sections there will be some reflection on the potential links with behaviour.

While this chapter has been laid out in two sections for ease of reading, it must be emphasized that there is no such division between mind, heart, body and soul. They are all intertwined in a dynamic interplay as we act, interact and react within our particular emotional, social and physical environment. The emphasis in this section is also going to be on the significance of the senses in contributing how we literally as well as metaphorically understand who we are and our place in the world, rather than the biological intricacies of how the senses work.

The first part, about the brain, also carries a health warning! This is because although the information I want to share with you is as up to date as possible at the time of writing (2009), nevertheless in the interval between writing and publishing, some new discovery will probably have been made that makes neuroscientists rethink what they have told us. It is rather like the information about 'healthy eating' which seems to change on a regular basis – although unfortunately lots of chocolate still has a downside – a little apparently is alright.

Part 1: The brain

In order to understand the potential impact of experience and thereby the ongoing effect on behaviour, we first need to have an understanding of the workings of the brain, but first there are a number of key points to consider:

- The brain is possibly the most complex structure in the universe and our understanding of it is still in its infancy, in spite of the enormous strides in recent times in untangling some of its processes.
- The mind is embedded in the workings of the brain, but exactly how the processes of an organic structure evolve into the miracle of our understanding of a personal 'self' remains an ongoing mystery.
- It is generally agreed that the fastest period of brain growth is in the first four years or so of life, with the growth in the first year to eighteen months perhaps being particularly dynamic (Matsuzawa et al., 2001; Knickmeyer et al., 2008).
- The brain has time-related surges in development which roughly correspond with periods of significant shifts in skills and abilities.[1] The early years contain a number of these surges, with another significant 'wave' occurring in adolescence.[2]
- The brain itself is a product of millennia of evolution in humans just as in other mammals and so many of its basic structures and allied functions are similar to those of other species.
- Contrary to some earlier perspectives on brain development, 'new neural connections in response to experience can be made across the lifespan', (Siegel, 2003). In other words, we can adapt and change ways of thinking and behaviour over time.
- The brain has areas of specialization which appear to deal with different types of information such as vision, emotion, memory, learning, hearing and so on, but it is also an *associative* organ, bringing together and combining sensory and emotional information which *both shapes and is shaped by* cognitive levels of the interpretation of experience. This forms the 'complete picture' that we experience in our day-to-day lives.
- The human brain optimally survives and builds on a continuous stream of information from both body and environment, but too much or too little information can cause stress in one form or another.
- At birth the brain is 'the most undifferentiated of any "organ" in the body' (Siegel, 2003, 2007).
- The right hemisphere is more advanced than the left from about the twenty-fifth gestational week until early into the second year of life (Schore, 1994, 2003).
- While our genetic inheritance provides the information for the brain's structure, function and how it grows and matures, it is *experience* which ultimately influences the way in which the brain is uniquely 'wired' for each individual. As LeDoux (1998) puts it, 'nature and nurture are partners in our emotional life'.
- Areas of the brain that mediate what are termed 'executive functions' – i.e. planning, organizing, self-monitoring, problem solving, sequencing – mature later than those areas of the brain that mediate our more fundamental functions and our emotions.
- The different areas in the brain grow and mature at different rates, culminating in full maturity in the twenties – although the brain continues to adapt to experience through the lifespan.

- The newborn baby's brain already has a 'uniquely complex anatomy . . . with all major systems present in various stages of immaturity' (Gregory, 2004).

With all this in mind, we now turn to some information about the brain itself.

The brain's basic structure and function

As noted above, the human brain is a combination of *genetic information* in the way it is structured and its components organized and *experience* which 'fine tunes' the circuitry between the various areas of the brain – so basically our brains are all the same and, at the same time, uniquely different. Development obviously starts in the womb, for example as early as the seventeenth to twentieth day of gestation, when the tiny, primitive embryo develops what is termed the 'neural plate'. By the twenty-third day, a structure called the 'neural groove' appears and the edges begin to curl up and after a further two days meet at the top to form a tube which is the start of the whole nervous system.

The third week of gestation is a very busy time for our growing baby as the beginnings of eyes and ears are starting to be formed, a rudimentary heart starts to beat, and at the top or 'head end' of the neural tube three vesicles are formed which will ultimately become the different areas of the brain, i.e. the forebrain, midbrain and hind brain. In many texts you will find that these areas are also given wonderfully evocative names, for example, the hind brain is also termed the *rhombencephalon*, but I will persist with more straightforward (though perhaps more boring) terms.[3]

The mysterious beauty of the organization of all the cells in the body to their ultimate destinations continues during gestation. The secrets of exactly how this migration of cells occurs have not yet been uncovered, but what appears to happen is that in these early weeks and months the cells must travel to their final location and settle down. The cells can then begin to make the early connections which will allow the baby to emerge as a fully functioning newborn. However, like an orchestra tuning up for the full concert, these cells are waiting for the experiences which will combine with the baby's genetic structure and temperament to play their part in shaping the person that the baby will become. Because of the sheer 'openness' of the early developing brain, it is obvious that the quality and type of experiences that we encounter will influence how these neural patterns are laid down, for good or ill. How the brain is 'constructed' also provides more information as to why early experiences provide such a solid framework for the way we feel, think about and react to our world.

The evolutionary neuroanatomist Dr Paul MacLean[4] put forward a theory that we have not one brain but three, reflecting both our evolutionary history and our links with other species. All these parts of the brain intermingle and communicate but their development, structure and focus of attention, so to speak, is governed by their adaptations in our distant past. How the brain develops in the womb and postnatally echoes these ancient patterns laid down in response to our needs for survival. These needs include not only the necessity for breathing, for our hearts to beat and for us to digest our food, but also to communicate and *be with* others.

In essence, the brain is mainly developed from the 'bottom up' and so the oldest (in evolutionary terms) structures are formed the earliest. The areas identified earlier as hindbrain, midbrain and forebrain evolve into the structures more usually identified with and broadly analogous to the brain stem (also sometimes referred to as the 'reptilian brain') and which includes the *cerebellum* (see below), the midbrain (also the 'mammalian brain,' 'subcortical', 'emotional brain') and the two hemispheres of the cortex respectively (Sunderland, 2006). Our first look is therefore at the 'reptilian' brain.

The brain stem or 'reptilian brain'

At birth, it is this 'reptilian' brain stem that is fully developed. Contained within what is a very compact space are complex groups of nuclei with intricate systems of pathways. These structures are said to be involved in arousal, attention, cardiac reflexes, swallowing, sleep, regulating awareness and relaying nerve signals to the cerebral cortex. Such findings in these subcortical regions of the brain point to areas in the brain supportive of emotional processing and provide part of the evidence linking sensory information, the development of processing 'circuits' and ultimately individual responses. It also strongly reinforces the notion that the newborn is already 'primed' for interaction with the world.

The brain stem is also involved with evolutionary safeguards against *danger*, i.e. the newborn infant can show a 'startle' reflex and begin to cry if feeling unsafe or placed alone on a cold surface. This response to a possible threat to survival is therefore entrenched in the human brain at its very oldest and deepest level, and a very interesting perspective is supplied by Lewis et al. (2000). They note that echoes of the territorial displays by many species, including reptiles, who attack and repel possible intruders can be seen in the actions of gang members who 'mark their domains' equally strongly and attack and repel those who 'don't belong'. Outsiders are seen as a threat and therefore dangerous, and the response is equally stark.

Quartz and Sejnowski (2002) cite a study in the 1950s where two groups of boys were invited to spend three weeks in a summer camp. Each group didn't know about the presence of the other at first and the idea behind the 'experiment' was that after a week or so, the boys would be invited to take part in some competitive games when 'hostility' might emerge. In reality, it didn't take long for the boys to see the 'other' group as 'enemies' and mayhem generally ensued, with any intrusion onto particular territory fiercely resisted long before any opportunity for the competitive games.[5]

While such behaviour is undoubtedly troubling, we must also reflect on similar aspects which appear to be part of ordinary life. For example, it is notable that at sporting events, fans tend to stay within their own groups with specific insignia such as scarves and team colours that clearly designate to which group they belong. In addition, teams often have a particular space at their home ground in which they usually sit. In fact, I would suggest that many of us have an urge for a space which is our own, usually our home or even a room or area within a room. This means that we can feel threatened – no matter how mildly – if we perceive that our space is invaded in some way. Also in the workplace we may have a particular chair or part of the office which is 'ours', and even guarding our 'own' mug. Those who work in open plan offices can mark out their territory too by a range of soft toys, a plant or strategically placed box of tissues, pens and photos.

Such a desire therefore appears to have very deep roots indeed, and may go some way to helping us understand when a child might appear to overreact to what may seem a unthreatening 'invasion' of their space to an observing adult. However, to the child, such an intrusion may resonate with these deep-seated and ancient desires for an area which is 'theirs'. It may also go some way to explaining why sharing – an attribute which is top of the list for most early years' practitioners for children to acquire – is so difficult. We are giving away some of our 'territory' – and we don't do it lightly.

Thinking further about the need for a space in which we feel safe may also contribute in some part to understanding the power of attachment needs. To feel loved and cared about means that there is space in the mind of another, and if we feel that somehow that space is being taken over we can become highly distressed. In young children it may be the pain of sharing attention with a new sibling, while in an adult it may be the pain of jealousy when witnessing the loved one appearing to share their feelings with another. Our territory of love has also been invaded.

The 'mammalian'/subcortical/emotional/limbic brain

In the subcortical part of the brain, enveloped by the cortex, lies the 'limbic' or 'emotional' brain which drapes around the brain stem in a semblance of a rim. Among its folds are crucial structures which include the *amygdala*, the *thalamus, hypothalamus* and *hippocampus*. This part of the brain increasingly, over time, becomes more intertwined with what can be termed the 'thinking' or 'logical' brain, but it has to be noted that the strong connections between these structures and the cortex are very much a 'two-way process' and, as we know, our emotions can frequently 'override' logic. In fact, emotions are the powerhouse that drives behaviour, even in those circumstances which may seem the most logical, such as choosing a bank offering the best interest rate. These structures (and others within this limbic system)[6] form part of that neural 'clothesline' on which we peg most of our decisions.

Now follows some information about those key structures mentioned above, starting with the *amygdala*, which has strong connections with the hippocampus, thalamus, hypothalamus, sensory cortex, prefrontal cortex and brain stem and has been implicated in many studies as playing a crucial role in the processing of emotions, especially fear and anxiety. It is especially interesting as, according to Cozolino (2006), the amygdala has already reached a 'high degree of maturity by the eighth month of gestation, allowing it to associate a fear response to a stimulus prior to birth' (p.57). Linking this information with its further maturation at birth and its role in the assessment of danger, responses and emotions there is a strong indication that the baby is already 'primed' for awareness of threat in any form. In particular, parts of the amygdala appear to be directly linked to the autonomic nervous system (which can either speed up or slow down bodily functions) allowing for immediate response to a sense of danger.

Overall the amygdala appears to be a 'key component of emotional memory *throughout life*; it associates survival value, based on experience with the object of the senses', (Cozolino, 2006, p.164, my emphasis). Links with the sensory system are also strongly implicated as information appears to feed into the amygdala. The different sensory systems themselves all have a different pattern of connections and so it seems that it is the amygdala that pulls all the information together, as Damasio (1999) implies.

If we make further links with the knowledge that babies are sensitive to the emotional expressiveness of faces and that such a reaction is 'hardwired' into the human brain, this provides strong support for the impact of the quality of experience on the infant and especially the need for comfort when the baby is distressed – because for the baby something which causes distress is a potential 'threat'. We can also link this awareness of threat with Crittenden's (1999) view on the development of the attachment relationship, i.e. that it is a defence against *danger*.

The *thalamus* has an essential role in that it appears to be the 'relay station' for sensory information (apart from smell and possibly taste). It also may play another role in the way in which different cortical areas emerge during foetal development. Work done by Schlagger and O'Leary of the Salk Institute (in Bear et al., 1996, p.492) demonstrated that it may be information relayed through the thalamus that specifies the formation of different areas in the cortex. This prenatal role, if proved, would link logically with the role of sensory relay station taken by the thalamus postnatally.

The *hypothalamus* is strongly connected to the brain stem and the frontal lobes (see below) as well as to those other structures mentioned in this section. It has centres within it that are involved in sexual function, the autonomic nervous system, hormonal secretion, temperature regulation in the body and appetite. If we reflect on these functions and link them with our understanding of emotions, it becomes clearer how much our bodily/sensory experiences contribute to our understanding of what is an emotion and how we then evaluate (make meaning of) what those sensations mean to us as individuals. For example, 'butterflies in the stomach' can mean anxiety, excitement and/or fear dependent on the context and the individual's own particular attitude towards that context based on previous experience.

The hypothalamus also plays an important part in what is termed 'the HPA-axis', i.e. the links between the *h*ypothalamus, the *p*ituitary and *a*drenal glands, in times of stress as these structures together regulate the production of *cortisol*, which is produced by humans in response to stressful situations (Karr-Morse and Wiley, 1997; Gunnar, 1998; Panksepp, 1998; Sunderland, 2006).

The *hippocampus* has three layers and several parts. It is particularly associated with memory formation, especially short-term memory. This is crucial, as without this we would be unable to 'lay down' long-term memories nor, would we be able to function from one moment to the next as we would constantly be experiencing each moment as 'new'. It also has an important role in how we understand our spatial relationships within our environment.[7] There are strong connections to and from the amygdala and related sensory memories of smell and taste. Incidentally, the hippocampus is not only strongly involved in the processes of encoding memories but also in retrieving them.

Overall, it is the limbic system which appears to act as both filter and coordinator of the streams of information coming both from the 'internal body environment' as Lewis et al. (2000) put it, and sensory information from the external environment. Its effects can be immediate with changes in heart rate, breathing patterns and skin reactions, such as sweating or the feeling of hairs 'standing up' on the back of the neck. Other effects can be more long-term, such as changes in hormonal outputs and the workings of the immune system. The limbic system also has an effect on configuring our facial muscles to make up those ultimately universally recognizable facial expressions we use to communicate our feelings and sensations to the outside world.

Perry (2006) reminds us that the workings of the brain stem and limbic system work outside of our awareness and it is at this level of brain functioning that 'the actual effective sensation of fear arises'. He goes onto say that 'only after communication with cortical areas (see below) is the individual able to make the more complex cognitive associations that allow interpretation of this internal state of anxiety' (p.33).

What we will discover when we move onto emotions, relationships and interactions is that it is the quality of our relationships that help establish these limbic-cortical connections and that these are still very much in progress in the young child. A child's reactions to something that seems threatening to them will be embedded in these ancient, neurological systems with only the earliest beginnings of being able to 'rationalize' the validity or otherwise of the possible threat they encounter.

The cortex (or cerebrum) – those hemipsheres

The cortex – the final frontier of human brain evolution – is divided into two connected hemispheres which in turn have four lobes termed the *frontal, parietal, temporal* and *occipital* lobes. Certain major functions are generally accepted to be associated with each of these areas:

- The frontal lobe, and in particular the pre-frontal lobe, appears to deal with the most abstract and complex of brain functions, for example thinking, planning and conceptualizing, and in the conscious 'appreciation' of emotion – those 'executive functions'.
- The parietal lobe appears to be mainly involved with movement, orientation, calculation and 'certain types of recognition', somatic sensation and body image.
- The temporal lobe deals with hearing, language, comprehension, sound and some aspects of memory and emotion.
- The occipital lobe is mostly taken up with visual processing areas.

The cortex has a specialized structure in that it is composed of six layers or sheets of neurons working from the bottom up, so level 6 or VI is at the bottom and level 1 or I is at the top. Within these layers, the cells that are responsive to similar inputs are arranged in columns that cut across all of the layers; such columnar patterns are seen in other structures in the brain, such as in the visual cortex. This columnar organization of cells in the cortex means that connections between the neurons can go in both directions, between layers, upwards and downwards and deep into the hidden structures of the brain. It is fascinating to note that when children start to build, they often do so first in columns.

The pre-frontal cortex, the part of the brain at the very front, accounts for around 29 per cent of the total cortex in humans compared to 7 per cent in the dog, for example, providing us with a suggestion as to the importance of this part of the brain. This prefrontal cortex also has various key areas including the orbital pre-frontal cortex (the bit just above the eyes), which is seen by Schore and others as that part of the brain particularly important for the social/emotional/regulation circuit alluded to above. The pre-frontal cortex as a whole is described by Goldberg (2001) as 'probably the best connected part of the brain' and seems to be directly interconnected with every important structure we have discussed.[8]

Goldberg's view is shared by Siegal (2007), who notes that the middle pre-frontal cortex links 'the body, brainstem, limbic, cortical and social processes into one functional whole' (p.38). Goldberg, incidentally, very much focuses in his book on the cognitive role of the frontal cortex, especially the pre-frontal cortex. However, when he speaks of trauma, disease or dysfunction in these lobes he describes how 'patients are emotionally disinhibited'. In particular he notes that: 'their ability to inhibit the urge for instant gratification is extremely impaired. They do what they feel like doing when they feel like doing it without any concern for social taboos or legal prohibitions. They have no foresight of the consequences of their actions'. (p.139).

If we link Goldberg's generally strongly cognitive approach with what others (e.g. Schore, Perry, Panksepp and Sunderland) who are perhaps more attuned to how we learn social skills and our emotional well-being are saying about the development of the connections between the limbic system and the frontal cortex, we can begin to see parallels between what Goldberg describes and the 'uninhibited' behaviour of babies and very young children. Children have to *learn* to inhibit or control their impulses to do what they want in some situations, and it can be seen that children need strong support in making those connections in order to be able to do so. Without such help children may grow but not 'grow up', as Perry puts it. Incidentally, Goldberg does, in fact, refer to Schore's work with a degree of wonder and admiration at his 'provocative hypothesis' regarding the importance of early mother–infant interaction in shaping this part of the brain so involved with social maturity.

We now take a step 'sideways' to reflect on early development and the growth of the ability to inhibit behaviour with another intriguing notion, which is that we need to experience physically what we can then abstract as a 'concept'. The first 'sideways step' is an example provided by Goldberg from his mentor Alexander Luria. Luria asked adult patients with frontal lobe dysfunction to do the *opposite* of what he was demonstrating, e.g. when Luria raised his fist, the patient had to raise their finger and vice versa. These patients had great difficulty doing this, and this brought to my mind those difficulties that children aged around four years have in imitating actions involving 'crossover', i.e. the adult touches their left ear with the right hand and children tend to touch the left ear with the left hand, (Gattis et al., 2002).

Although this tendency to use an ipsilateral (same side) rather than a contralateral action had been observed in earlier research and hypothesized to be because of brain lateralization or because children want to use a 'favoured' hand, Gattis and her colleagues, in their research, thought that this tendency was more to do with children understanding the *goal* of the intended action. Therefore the children imitated what they perceived as the *purpose* of the observed action. However, it may also be possible that *the capacity to inhibit* their natural inclination to do what may have seemed sensible rather than be able to imitate the action as requested is immature at this age, thereby making it more difficult to follow the precise instruction.

The other example of needing to experience something physically before we can understand a concept comes from Reddy (2008), who notes that children need to have a proper understanding of the reality of the space behind them before they can understand 'past' in the context of time. You may be wondering how these all link together, but the suggestion is that we need to experience being 'inhibited' before we can begin to develop an ability to inhibit ourselves, and that we need to understand the properties of the physical world and understand that we have a physical self before we can begin to understand boundaries – a hypothesis to be discussed further in later chapters, but now we turn back to the brain.

Two halves – one brain

Physiologically, the two cerebral hemispheres are not absolute mirror images of each other, with the right frontal lobe being somewhat wider than the left while in the area at the back (the occipital lobe) it is the other way round, with the left occipital lobe being somewhat wider than the right. There are also some biochemical differences, with receptors for some neurochemicals being more prevalent in one hemisphere than another.

Interestingly, and fascinatingly too, Trevarthen (2004) notes that the asymmetry in areas of the brain can already be discerned in foetal development. He particularly cites those areas in the left hemisphere which are essential for 'language understanding in the great majority of adult humans'. These appear already to have a different formation to comparable areas on the right at twenty-four weeks' gestational age, with the implication that the 'human brain is set to acquire some language long before it hears a single word' (p.126). However, this readiness for language may also be linked to the awareness of the foetus to his/her mother's voice heard in the womb. This has been illustrated by research which demonstrated how babies appear to recognize and prefer the sound of their mother's voice soon after birth – something which will be discussed further in Chapter 3.

What is also of note is that the right and left sides of the brain appear to have different but complementary functions, so while structures on the right and left side are broadly reflective of each other, their 'focus of attention' can be slightly different. Overall the right hemisphere appears to be biased towards emotional processing (especially more negative affect), self-awareness, facial recognition, bonding/attachment and global analysis, while the left appears to be more biased towards facts, analysis, awareness of others and more positive affect (Cozolino, 2006). It is even the left side of the amygdala which appears to be the most active when an unfamiliar face is viewed and is perhaps being assessed (i.e. analysed) as to whether it is friend or foe.

Trevarthen (2004) also suggests that the right side of the brain, with its greater activity at birth and into the second year, appears to lay down the foundations for its greater superiority in 'perception of form, in visuo-constructive skills . . . and habits of interpersonal and co-operative life' (p.126). The extensive work of Alan Schore (2003) has also emphasized the importance of the right hemisphere for the 'unconscious processing of socioemotional information, the regulation of bodily states, the capacity to cope with emotional stress and the corporeal and emotional self' (p.113)[9]. The right side of the brain also appears to play an important role in attachment formation, and again it is interesting to note that the long period of greater activity of the right brain matches the development of this important relationship.

What we need to consider when thinking about children's behaviour in a developmental context is the knowledge of these growth spurts with the right side of the brain being more dominant in the first eighteen months to two years until the left hemisphere shows a growth spurt starting around the end of this period – incidentally tying in with a surge in verbal language. These alternating growth spurts continue until approximately puberty, when the brain undergoes a period of great reorganization with growth spurts, chemical changes, for example in sleeping patterns, and emotional shifts and changes all occur. These alternating periods may help us think about what *types* of learning may be the general focus for the developmental needs of the child.

The links between right hemisphere dominance from birth until around the second year, the development of highly important links with those parts of the brain which allow for thinking and reflection and the quality of the child's emotional experiences during that time cannot be stressed enough. Schore (2003) goes so far as to suggest that the attachment relationship 'thus directly shapes the maturation of the infant's right brain . . .', the 'ultimate product of this social-emotional development is a particular system in the prefrontal areas of the right brain that is capable of regulating emotions' (p.113). Interestingly, the right frontal cortex tends to be thicker than the left. It is important to emphasize that these pathways or systems are developed in response to the child's emotional environment, so that a child who is nurtured, protected, loved, talked to and played with will develop circuits that lay a foundation for well-being and emotional health. It is true, as Gerhardt (2004) put it, that love certainly does matter.

Communication between the spheres

As each side of the body is 'controlled' by the contra-lateral side of the brain, communication between the two halves is imperative. The major connection is the *corpus callosum*, where much of the communication between hemispheres is transmitted. Goddard (2005) stresses that communication between the two hemispheres is essential 'for all academic learning' and is, of course, essential for 'balancing' the different aspects of information reaching the brain second by second.

Early studies on rats by Denenberg et al. (in Fox and Davidson, 1984), suggest that handling of these animals promoted development of the corpus callosum 'just as it does for other systems in the body'. These very early findings, supported by later research on nurturing and grooming in rats, especially on the action of brain chemicals such as oxytocin, could potentially suggest that the amount of handling/touching that most babies encounter in their daily life may also contribute to appropriate human development of the corpus callosum. It therefore does not seem too strong a leap to suggest that babies who, for whatever reason, do not receive such handling may have subsequent difficulties in the integration of information not only physically but also psychologically, because being licked and groomed probably feels nice to the baby rat and being held does appear to feel good to humans. The years of research by Meaney et al. (1999) – and quoted extensively by Begley (2007)[10] – on rats noted that the 'handled' rats produced less stress hormones and were generally 'more exploratory, less fearful and less reactive to stress when they are adults'.

Alternatively, a child who resists or is unresponsive to being held, bathed cuddled or hugged, may set the scene where such care may become less timely and/or responsive, and so a cycle of non-responsiveness/resistance and reduced nurturing could be established. For example, St. Clair et al. (2007) note that 'if parents regularly attempt to engage with a child who, for whatever reason does not respond to social cues, they will adjust their behaviour accordingly and will eventually cease to expect or wait for such a response' (p.23).

In addition, the baby who is described as having a 'difficult' temperament, such as being hard to soothe – or even *perceived* as being hard to soothe – may be at greater risk of adverse caretaking if parents are already having problems empathizing and thinking about the baby as an individual with needs and/or if they are overwhelmed by their own needs. These ideas are supported again by Meaney's rat research, where he found that baby rats born to stressed mothers who were then 'adopted' by comforting and stable rat mums were 'indistinguishable' as adults in their behaviour from baby rats reared by their loving parent. Sadly, the opposite was also true, establishing that in rats nurture was a powerful influence on later development. The links with human experience are very strong, as we shall see when we discuss interactions.

How does the brain grow?

It has been well established that the fastest period of brain growth (as far as is known to date) is within the first four years, and as said earlier, the first eighteen months to two years are suggested to be the most dynamic within this phase of growth. We also have to appreciate that overall, while primate studies show similar developmental rates in all cortical regions, the rates of development in humans vary. Such differences between human and primate brain development may reflect perhaps the more complex range of human functioning.[11] We have seen above that there are surges in growth at different times, in different areas and with different emphasis. For example, Siegel (2007) considers that 'the period between 3 and 7 years of age appears to be a profoundly important time for the acquisition of executive attentional functions raising the notion that interventions may be best initiated at this time' (p.115). It is interesting to note that this suggestion reinforces the idea that children are beginning to be able to shift their focus of attention from themselves to that of others with growing (but still very early and vulnerable) understanding of the different thoughts and needs of others during this period.

The actual growth of the brain in any area is made up of the brain cells themselves actually getting bigger; the second aspect of growth is the proliferation of connections between the cells, which are further discussed below; and lastly by the process of *myelination*, which is the formation of a fatty coat along the information conduit of the cell – of which more later.

It is also true that the study of brain maturation is ongoing and there is much that is not known. However, Gur (2005), in a review of brain maturation studies, suggests three generally accepted findings:

1   there is a 'large variability in the rate of maturation among brain regions';
2   'people are not biologically prepared to exercise mature frontal lobe control until they reach adulthood';
3   the main index of maturation is the rate of myelination.

Association areas

Within the broad hemispheric divisions or lobes identified above, there are further subdivisions: primary sensory areas, the motor areas, secondary sensory areas and the association areas. The primary sensory and motor areas are those that initially receive signals from the ascending sensory and motor pathways, while the secondary areas between these primary areas allow for information to move between the main lobes. For example, areas within the temporal and parietal lobes that receive information from one of the vision areas (which lie mainly in the occipital lobe) are termed 'secondary visual' (sensory) areas. It is in the remainder of the cortex, particularly in the frontal and temporal lobes, that are found what are termed the 'association areas', and these seem to be those that are most involved in our 'higher' and more uniquely human capabilities. However, 70–80 per cent of the brain's activity appears to be dedicated to processing sensory information, which stresses the importance of information from the senses. If this is the case, then the implication here is that any particular dysfunction in sensory processing in one or more areas is potentially going to have a greater overall impact on the eventual manifestation of outward behaviour.

The 'other brain' – the cerebellum

At the back of the brain stem lies the cerebellum which, while ultimately smaller than the 'cerebrum' nevertheless contains more neurons than the two hemispheres put together (Bear et al., 1996) and it's 'anatomy parallels in miniature the anatomy of the whole brain' (Goldberg, 2001). At birth it is large, complex and very immature with development occurring mainly postnatally, with the fastest period of growth being between birth and fifteen months and generally with a 'faster rate than the cortex' between birth and four years of age. Studies by Knickmeyer et al. (2008) point to a growth in cerebellar volume of *240 per cent* in the first year, which may reflect the rapid growth in the motor abilities and balance of the baby during this time. Maturation then appears to continue at a much slower rate until around fifteen years (Goddard, 2005).

The cerebellum also develops strong connections with the frontal lobe and the limbic (emotional) system. Incidentally, the left cerebellum has also been noted to be activated for fearful faces, and disturbance in the cerebellum has been put forward as part of the aetiology for autism. This finding provides a further dimension in that the cerebellum may not only influence spatial processing but also impact on how such sensory information may be experienced subjectively if this structure does have a key role in emotions. There is also a growing understanding of how movement itself influences learning (Berthoz, 2000; Goddard, 2005) – providing an example of the links between different areas of development.

Recent research on the role of the cerebellum is pointing to complex and wide-ranging functions such as short-term memory, learning new skills, spatial awareness and sequencing in addition to its long-established association with motor development and control. Researchers such as Stoodley and Stein (2009) also suggest that the cerebellum may be part of a neural network impairment in dyslexia, while Levin (2009) considers the role of the cerebellum in emotions.

Those little grey cells

Those of you who are fans of Agatha Christie, especially her stories involving Hercule Poirot, the little Belgian detective, will remember how much stress he places on the workings of his 'little grey cells', and indeed in the human brain literature there is reference to grey matter and white matter. Grey matter refers to the cells themselves, while white matter refers to the process of myelination already mentioned.

So, those little grey cells are the 'building blocks' of the brain, termed *neurons*. The crucial aspect is how they connect with each other and what aspects of neuronal growth impact on the ability within each human being to function. It is these processes that contribute to the 'fine tuning' that allows for the differences between individual brains within the basic overall architecture. In the brain there are approximately a 100–200 billion neurons, *each* of which is capable of receiving up to 10,000 connections.[12] The activity in the brain in the early years is immense, illustrated by the uptake of glucose, the brain's main fuel, being particularly high in the first two years of life. In addition, studies that measure the rates of glucose metabolism in the frontal cortex between ages two and four years lend support to the findings of the high growth rates in the frontal circuits between the ages of three to six years, which further supports the implication that any trauma, delay or dysfunction may be particularly compounded during these formative years. A study by Johnston (1995), who as well as reinforcing the information that synapses are produced in 'greater than adult numbers by postnatal age 2 years', also points out that particular glutamate[13] receptors are 'opened more easily' and 'for a longer period than adult channels'. Such receptors play an important role in *long-term potentiation*, which is the long-lasting strengthening of the connections between brain cells. This suggests that in the first two years of life, the neurons themselves are *literally* more open to experience – the downside being that brain function is also more vulnerable to all types of adversity during this period, including both under and over stimulation.

Another study by Filippi et al. (2002) of children with developmental delay aged both under and over two years found that in children *over* two years there were changes in specific neurotransmitter ratios, in particular brain structures compared to controls. Those *under* two years did not show these changes. This potentially implies that as these children grew older, experience was being processed differently and, additionally, developmental delay was having an accumulative effect over time, leading to the alteration in the neurotransmitter ratios. These findings emphasize the idea that as the brain continues to mature any dysfunction is compounded as the brain tries to organize new experiences *within increasingly idiosyncratic parameters.*

Back to basics

The basic neuron consists of three main parts. The cell body itself stores genetic material and makes proteins and any other substances essential for the cells survival. The other parts of the basic neuron identify the main differences between neurons and other bodily cells: they directly communicate with each other and are designed to do so, i.e. by the addition of two other structures, which are essentially nerve fibres – the dendrites and the axon. Fundamentally, the dendrites are 'receivers' and the axon is the 'output' channel. It is these axons that carry information to other cells and can vary enormously in length (even several feet) depending on function. Neurons can also differ depending on, for example, which layer of the cortex they are in and the type and number of connectors they have, but all nevertheless follow the same basic pattern.

While the functional localization of brain structures is roughly similar in all humans, the knowledge that different brain areas mature at different rates, coupled with 'wiring' in response to individual experience, means that information is organized within each person in a unique way. The neurons themselves tend to be organized into groups, which appear to link with each other in patterns sometimes termed 'neural nets'. This in turn creates circuits of information, which may be adjacent to one another but also in different parts of the brain.

What is so fascinating about the way neurons 'talk' to one another, and which adds to the incredible complexity, is that the information from one to the next is carried by chemicals known as 'neurotransmitters' – and glutamate has already been mentioned. Others include some well researched chemicals such as dopamine, serotonin, oxytocin, cortisol and opiods but there are many more. These provide the means of information transmission across the minute gaps, called synapses, between the neurons, but their function is more complex than simply transmitting the information as they can also *inhibit* information.

Another twist to the tale is that different neurons can have 'receptors' for different neurotransmitters, and the numbers of receptors to specific chemicals can also vary in different parts of the brain. This is why it is often difficult to compare the actions of some drugs with others, as they have a variable effect dependent on the type of drug, the chief chemical component within the drug, what its main action is and what side effects can also occur. Neural activity in the brain is by electrical impulse and neurotransmitters provide the necessary links between neurons but their effects vary dependent on what is happening both to and within the person at any one time.

Studies that have examined these chemical changes have shown up the different types of chemical activity in different locations which, in turn, help to sort out the anatomical patterns made by the myriad connections between the cells. It is these 'maps' of activity that have provided the clues to the dawning realization that it is 'environmental stimuli' that shapes and alters these maps and that this type of organization within the brain is especially sensitive in the early years of development, and so a picture is emerging of why experiences are so crucial in childhood.

If you have seen a copy of Michaelanelo's painting *The Creation of Adam* on the ceiling of the Sistine Chapel in Rome (or been fortunate enough to have seen it in person), the finger of God is reaching for the finger of Adam but they do not quite touch. This is a marvellous representation of that strange combination of both a space and a relationship which exists between neuron to neuron and is perhaps a reflection of the communication within a space that exists between one person and another. Even more fascinating perhaps is that the cloak depicted behind God in the painting has been thought to be a precise, anatomically correct representation of the human brain, which makes one wonder whether Michaelangelo had somehow intuitively surmised the existence of this eloquent space.

Myelination

A role crucial to brain maturation and function is a type of brain cell known as 'glia', and these outnumber neurons by 10:1. Glial cells provide layers of fatty membrane to insulate the axons; this process has already been mentioned, i.e. *myelination*. These layers provide a 'wrap-around' structure which covers the 'messenger' part of the neuron (the axon) and allows for the more efficient transmission of the electrical signals. Myelinated axons transmit information at approximately 100 times faster than an unmyelinated axon which transmits a much 'fuzzier' signal. This has implications for the quality and speed of processing in any particular developmental domain. The implication for early development is that the myelination process is part of that complex maturation of the brain which takes place, as we have already noted, both over time *and* at different rates in different areas of the brain (Benes et al., 1994; Paus et al., 1999). These findings point to an association between the quality of processing information and the age of the individual which, if we link to the immaturity of the child's brain and their ability to understand, process and respond to our requests, instructions and information, indicates that children may take time to work out what we want.

Pruning

In the first two to three years or so, millions of connections are made between neurons, unformed and then reformed dependent on experience, including emotional experience. For example, the visual cortical neurons in the infant have one and a half times as many synapses as do the neurons in adults. This amazing 'rampage' of connections then undergoes a process of pruning which, incidentally, does begin prenatally to some extent. During periods of rapid growth, multiple connections are made and then as patterns of experience emerge, unused and/or unwanted connections between the brain cells are pruned away or wither. We are then left with a 'template' of responses in both physical and psychological realms. Sunderland (2006) notes that 'synaptic pruning' overall begins at around two years.

The enormous surges in connectivity that occur in these early years begin to slow down around the age of seven years. This coincides with greater areas of myelination in the brain as pathways/connections/patterns are strengthened and so are more permanently fixed in place, refining the way information is transmitted to the various structures in the brain.

Studies quoted by Locke (1995) also suggest that this overall process of connection and pruning is associated with periods of brain 'reorganization' which also appear to coincide with times of major transitions in development, including adolescence. Locke noted, for example, that both face and voice recognition appear to follow the same pattern of peaks and troughs of performance, including a 'dip' between the ages of ten to thirteen years (broadly) and then improved again starting at around age fourteen.

It may very well be that a major shift in development involving a significant change in some aspect of physical and/or psychological development may enhance, cause to plateau and even regress other aspects of development temporarily, and indeed this seems to be the generally pervading view of brain function (Fischer, 2005). However, once again it is experience that ultimately determines which synapses are pruned and which survive on a dynamic basis as well as at those times of reorganization and brain surge. Awareness of how brain activity is so high in the early years adds to the picture we are building of how *what* happens to the baby is so crucial.

The elastic/plastic brain?

You may have heard or read that the human brain is highly adaptable, and sometimes the term 'plasticity' is used – although the term is disliked by many neuroscientists. The human brain is certainly adaptable as humans, whatever their environment, can learn to live within their particular situation, but there are some caveats here. Adaptability, plasticity or elasticity is not infinite and can vary dependent on the particular areas of functioning and timing.

Nelson and Bosquet (2005) remind us that when thinking about how much the brain can be 'reorganised' by experience we need to take into account which areas of development we are talking about. For example, much of the research on how the brain adapts to trauma has been in the sensory and motor domains but, in contrast, little is apparently known about how emotional, social and learning pathways are altered. What must also be taken into account is that the immature, growing brain is more easily adaptable, which allows much hope for recovery from trauma, both physical and psychological. However, linking with what we already know about growth and pruning, the later such trauma may occur in any area of development, the harder it may become for change and adaptation to take place.

Summary

The new imaging technology which allows researchers and scientists to examine pictures of the living brain is providing support for both the existence of *broadly* specialized areas in the brain for different functions and that children and adults may use different areas for the same task, reinforcing a role for brain maturation (Johnson, 2001). *Emotions* are also interactive with brain maturation as well as *language, cognitive skills, movement* and *control over bodily functions*. At only a few hours old, babies will respond differently to happy, sad or surprised faces and are able to display facial, vocal and bodily signs of general contentment and distress which over the first year become more differentiated into joy, sadness, anger, fear and disgust (Soussignan and Schaal, 2005; Cozolino, 2006). More 'sophisticated' emotions, such as embarrassment and shame, are thought to enter the emotional stage at around fourteen months, tying in with the beginnings of a sense of 'ownership' both of body awareness and represented through the strong feelings evoked in children of this age by the ideas of 'me' and 'mine'. Schore (1994) provides evidence to suggest that this transition also reflects a change in the dominance of the cerebral hemispheres, which gradually moves from right to left in the early years, once language becomes the primary form of communication, and culminating in left-sided dominance for most people at around five to seven years. In contrast, both Trevarthen (2005) and Reddy (2005) consider that 'self-conscious' emotions such as shyness and 'showing off' appear in the first year.

There is one final bit of magic in the human brain and that is the discovery of 'mirror neurons', which are neurons that respond to the actions observed in another *as if* the individual was carrying out the action themselves. However, this is a topic which links very closely with research on imitation and so this wonderful capacity in the human brain will be discussed further in Chapter 3 where the main topic is interactions and relationships.

Part 2: Experiencing the world and getting to know the self

Now that we have discovered something about the brain, the next part of this chapter moves on to the way in which we being to understand and know the world, i.e. through the power of our senses and the information we derive through them. This means, of course, that we have to take into account that both the efficacy and maturation of each of our sensory systems may vary within individuals – not only with the more obvious such as those who are born deaf or blind or have major difficulties in movement, but to also consider that each of us may have slight variations in the way that all our senses work. For example, we may be particularly sensitive to sound or light or touch, or we may be someone who can tolerate lots of noise.

This means that when we consider the behaviour of children, we need to think about how are they actually experiencing their world at a sensory level – and children do provide clues in their attitudes and behaviour towards different types of stimuli. For example, I cannot wear jumpers made of lambswool as I find it too 'scratchy'; one friend hates loose clothing while another cannot bear anything that feels tight. We do not have these likes and dislikes linked to our senses only in adulthood but may already have a sensitivity in childhood, which may affect our reactions to what is offered to us to wear, to eat, to touch. Such sensitivities might also add to the power of a child's feelings when to coming into a noisy setting for the very first time. So now let us step into the world of our senses.

The kaleidoscope of the senses

What exists for the newborn baby? Without doubt, this new entrant into the world is already equipped with a range of skills and abilities as well as an intact, albeit immature, sensory system. In other words, the baby is able to smell, taste, feel, move, see and hear. She[14] is able to hear and recognize the sound of her parents' voices, especially her mother's, see the face of the parent at the magical distance between breast and face, vocalize through crying and other more gentle sounds, can grasp a finger tightly, move her feet in a stepping motion, root for the breast and suckle. She can also respond and react and, as noted earlier, throw her arms wide in a startle gesture when sensing some kind of danger – which for her in these early days is when her sensory systems will send an alarm call that will occur just as much when left alone as when experiencing discomfort, hearing a loud noise or experiencing sudden movements.

Overall, the senses within the brain are all composed of the same electrical impulses, but are ultimately experienced rather magically as individual senses (we know what we see, hear and feel etc.), as discrete entities *and* as a rich combination of our senses. For example, we can look at a beautiful view and be aware of the wind blowing on our faces, the feel of the sun on our skin, the sound of a bird calling, which all combine to produce the experience as it is felt holistically. It is as if the senses were all part of a wonderful kaleidoscope where all the parts continually shift into ever changing but exquisitely combined patterns of experience. However, for the newborn perhaps the picture is not quite so clear cut, and it may be that for babies there exists something akin to a phenomenon in adults known as 'synesthesia'. This is where one sensory pathway appears to combine with another. For example, some people can see a number and also a specific colour associated with that number, or associate some objects and sounds together. What seems to be emerging from studies quoted by Carter (2000), although not yet fully explained, is that babies may have similar patterns of sensory processing as that seen in people with synesthesia.

Initially, therefore, sensory experiences may be more globally experienced but become more specific and refined as the infant's body and brain mature in tandem. However, the senses themselves vary in their level of development at birth. For example, while smell and hearing are 'fully fledged' at birth, vision is not, and taste is confined to four basic tastes – sweet (breast milk is very sweet), sour, bitter and salt – although a fifth, (*umami* – *savoury*) has been discovered by Japanese researchers. This means that while infants have a 'kick-start' for experiencing the environment through their senses, the ongoing, moment by moment information needs organizing, and so, supported by experience, the different sensations begin to develop their particular pathways which allows humans to discriminate between what is heard, smelt, tasted and so on.

Sensory information itself covers a wide range and the particular brain areas involved in motor and sensory organization follow a well-organized pattern. For example, sensory nerves in the body enter the spinal cord towards the dorsal or 'back' side, while motor nerves exit from the ventral or 'front' side. The brain also follows this arrangement, with motor areas being towards the front, i.e. in the frontal lobes, whereas the sensory processes are concentrated 'more posteriorly in the occipital (vision), temporal (hearing) and parietal (touch) lobes' (Panksepp, 1998).

The senses themselves include the more commonly identified (i.e. vision, hearing, taste, touch and smell), but there is also the vestibular sense arising from the inner ear. This sorts out information about movement, gravity and balance – very important as babies and young children are placed in different positions by their adult carers and then, over time, independently become more mobile. This vestibular sense is allied to the proprioceptive sense, which provides information about body parts and body position.

Information also arises from internal organs (e.g. heart rate, blood pressure, breathing rate, bowel, bladder and stomach action, chemical changes in the blood and so on), much of which is unconscious except when the strength of a reaction to a situation brings such sensations into conscious awareness, for example a rapid heart rate when excited or fearful, 'butterflies' when anxious. Babies, while not 'metaware' of these sensations, i.e. will not recognize such feelings as indications of a particular emotion, will, nevertheless, experience bodily sensations in conjunction with particular contexts.

The information provided by the parent's responses to the baby's behaviour will provide a framework to organize their meaning. For example, the baby's discomfort will lead to crying or agitation, and parents may exaggerate a 'reflecting' response such as a profoundly sad face and then begin to soothe and comfort. Such interactions create ongoing, open-ended communication where the feelings of the baby are reflected by the parent. In this way, the baby is hopefully assisted to 'move on' to a more positive state or if the interaction is playful and fun, is enhanced with a matching and extending of the infant's joy. Ultimately, this helps the sensory and emotional systems to slowly become organized into a picture of what the world is like for the baby.

In the rest of this section, there is a brief overview of individual senses, starting with touch.

The importance of touch

Tactile information is different from information arising for example, from the eyes and ears in that the receptors are distributed throughout the body rather than in specialized locations. These receptors can respond to different types of stimuli, with the fundamental ones being touch, temperature, pain and body position, but there are a great many subdivisions of each of these; for example, the somatic system can differentiate between a blow or a pinprick and fingertips are so sensitive that a bump can be sensed that is 167 times smaller than the dot of Braille. The complexity of the task which the brain appears to do seamlessly can be grasped just from one example: bodies are finely tuned to changes in temperature and to the general experience of hot and cold. However, different parts of the human body appear to be more sensitive to either heat or cold but not both, and there are also small areas of skin between these 'hot and cold' spots which seem to be insensitive to either. This complexity of temperature maintenance and sensation gives some insight into why the newborn baby's 'temperature control' is not fully functional for a few weeks after birth, and they remain vulnerable to changes in temperature. We also have to remember that people have different responses to heat and cold, with some people being more sensitive to either. Linked with this is some indication mentioned previously that boys prefer lower temperatures than girls, so that a very warm group setting may be very uncomfortable for some boys who, if unable to verbalize or explain their discomfort, may simply become distressed or agitated. Similarly, very young girls may be feeling cold and again may become distressed, but again potentially unable to say why. Caldwell and Horwood (2008) also note that the tactile system in the head and face is different from that of the body, which means that some children may react to hair brushing/combing with great reluctance.

Touch itself also has profound emotional associations with the positive or negative feedback arising from the type of touch and handling the young child receives and the consistency of such approaches. We perhaps forget how much natural touching we do to babies and very young children, not just when holding, comforting and stroking but also when communicating directly with them. Parents and other adults often are holding the baby when talking to them, or if the baby is sitting or lying, parents will hold the baby's hands, stroke their face and so on. This all adds to the experience of being spoken to by providing something for the baby, a solid and tangible point of contact, while the baby listens to the sounds and watches the parent's face. As Caldwell and Horwood (2008) put it, the baby can 'feel' the communication as well as hear and see it. The emotional significance of the communication by touch remains with us throughout our lives as we respond to a hug, a pat on the shoulder, a hand hold – feeling through the skin the level of emotion in the mind and heart of the other.

We also need to be aware of how much we touch children when carrying out care and nurture routines such as nappy changing, and I wonder how often the *way* in which we carry out this simple care routine is linked with what it might *feel* like to the child. The length of time that some babies and very young children spend in group care naturally means that they will require their nappies to be changed at varying times during the day. Perhaps we need to reflect on the experience of the child during this intimate procedure when there may be nappy changing rotas or where whoever is available does the changing. This means that the child has to accommodate the different styles and approaches of a range of adults.

In addition, perhaps we also forget that adults are not interchangeable and everyone does things slightly differently. The different ways someone touches/handles a child will impact on the child's experience because some will use firm touching while others may use lighter touches. Incidentally, a lighter touch can be harder to localize and can also be more stimulating and alerting. The baby will have got used to how his mother does these care routines, so how someone else does it may cause passing distress until they become accustomed to this new way – and how much harder will this be if there are several people carrying out the activity? What impact might such experiences have on the child's developing sense of their body, and how they might relate and react to being held in the future?

Feeding a child also provides opportunities for closeness and physical contact. Again we might consider the impact for the sensory and emotional systems for the child if such feeding is rushed or the child is fed but generally not attended to, for example the adult is busy talking to someone else, watching television or preoccupied with their own thoughts.

Other links include the importance of touch in the promotion of the healthy development of the corpus callosum referred to earlier. Touch is also involved in *exploration* as touch is used to handle objects. Active touching includes pulling, lifting, stretching, squeezing, 'fingering' – all of which are in the baby's repertoire for exploration over time. The face is the most pressure sensitive part of the body, which is why we are so aware of a hair on our cheek for example. The other most sensitive parts of the body for the reception of touch are the fingers, the hands, the tip of the tongue and parts of the mouth – all areas heavily involved in very early exploration/ learning.

In addition, touching involves a *dual* experience for both what is being *touched* and what is being *felt*. For example, when the baby 'finds its feet' and enjoys the feeling of the feet in its mouth, the baby is not only receiving information from the mouth but also from the feet, thereby providing a knowledge of what 'my feet' feel like. It is interesting that this ability comes just before the time when many babies are beginning to support their weight (around six to eight months), allowing the brain to assimilate the familiar feeling of feet with the new sensation of feet to surface plus weight – thereby linking sensory information, movement and emotional feedback –whether the experience is positive or negative.

Recognizing the importance of touch and how it underpins much of early communication with its strong emotional overtones as well as its role in sensory and physical development means that we must pay respectful attention to our own attitudes towards touch. Not all adults are comfortable or confident handling and touching babies, and the very notion of touch has become imbued with the concerns over possible abuse. What should be instinctive, loving and respectful appears to have become something of a minefield for parents and other carers. We must try to balance being respectful to an individual child's responses to various levels of touch – not all children, especially if older, want or like hugs – respectful of situations and our own responses while at the same time fully acknowledging the profound human need for physical contact.

Vision

The visual system itself is highly complex and some of its functions are still poorly understood in spite of vast amounts of research. However, there are some key points to emphasize to add to the evidence for highly integrated functions both within and between developmental systems. The primary visual cortex is situated in the occipital lobe but as with all sensory information, processing passes through a number of stages and areas. The adult visual system takes many months, and in some parts years, before being fully functional. For example, the process of interconnectivity and pruning to 'define the fine structure of receptive fields to achieve the adult values of acuity and contrast sensitivity' appears to continue until the ages of three to four years (Atkinson, 2000). However, a newborn baby does appear to have a capacity for 'fairly sophisticated eye movements and has a good orientating system', but visual development overall is very rapid, particularly after the first six weeks of life (incidentally tying in with when the first smiles reliably appear) and which also suggest a period of adjustment to life outside the womb.

Atkinson (2000, p.119) states that:

> A number of early studies have claimed that spontaneous eye scanning patterns in new borns and 1 month olds are concentrated around the external contour of a pattern which produces maximum neural firing and also allows the infant to discriminate early on between objects.

Newborn vision is limited to orientating to single targets, especially faces, but this difficulty has fascinating consequences. First, it means that the baby's visual system is not overloaded with information, and second, the fact that the baby is mainly able to orientate to a single target means that baby is bound to spend long periods of time getting to know the face of their mother and other adults such as dad who might be closely involved with care. Through the immaturity of the visual system, by default almost, face-gazing becomes an integral part of the baby's experience. The baby, however, also needs to have some defence against gaze which may be too intense or when simply needing to 'call a halt' to an interaction, so being able to avert one's gaze is an important aspect of vision. Interestingly, this skill appears to link with the development of the frontal cortex, and people who have damage to parts of this structure appear to keep this fixated gaze.

By three months, vision appears to be sufficiently integrated for the baby to switch attention from one 'object' to another accompanied by a synonymous development of such systems as orientation, motion and colour awareness – incidentally all becoming more sensitive over time. For example, newborns and infants under one month appear to have very poor or absent colour discrimination. At six months an infant will illustrate a formidable integration of feature, form and location in space through recognition of people, and also around five to six months there is visual control of reach and grasp, pointing to awareness of 'near visual space'.

A child of this age can also usually adjust the shape of their hands to accommodate the shape of the desired object – a pattern which becomes established in our procedural, implicit (unconscious) memory system through the child's increasing desire and growing ability to reach and grasp. If we reach towards an object, we will notice how our fingers begin to adapt to its shape before we actually grasp it and is only inhibited with great difficulty. A child's ability to reach with one hand also appears to coincide with the child's control of the trunk, i.e. can sit steadily unsupported, which is usually around eight months.

Humans with forward facing eyes have binocular vision, i.e. what is seen is seen by both eyes simultaneously, but this is not yet 'working' in infants; the expectation is that at around seven to eight months the eyes will be working together. The key point is that:

> signals from the two eyes are sorted and combined so that those relating to stimuli in the same part of the visual field end up in the same part of the brain even if they arise in different eyes.
>
> (Derrington, 2002, p.147)

By one year there is visual control of locomotion, which indicates an integration of physical action, attention control and awareness of far and near visual space, and by eighteen months there is a wonderful integration of movement, speech and visual coordination as children can walk and carry an object at the same time and can direct where they want to go – vocalizing as they do so! Vision therefore is intimately linked with movement and not only helps us in knowing where we are going but also where we are in space in relation to other objects around us.

The links between the emotions and vision are also important. The experience of vision, or indeed the experience of any of the senses, exists, as Ramachandran (1999) describes, on two levels – the subjective experience and the objective 'third-person account' of what is there. This applies to whatever is seen. When a baby looks at the human face, the baby will actively see the face in the context of how well it can actually see and at the same time will experience a sensation dependent on both the expression on the face and how the baby is feeling itself – hot, cold, tired, lonely, playful, joyful. The face will become imbued with meaning and associations. In other words, there is a substantial, qualitative difference between how information is transmitted from the eye to the brain and what we eventually experience as 'seeing'. What is suggested is that the child's emotional 'view' of the world also influences to a greater or lesser degree, dependent on context, the peculiarly personal 'angle of perception' of visual experience.

Another aspect of vision which must be taken into account is light and colour. This has implications for behaviour too, as some children are sensitive to light. Elizabeth Jarman[15] and her wonderful work on 'communication-friendly spaces' has noted that many children do not respond well to fluorescent light and many settings can be far too 'busy', thereby overstimulating to some children whose behaviour may then reflect their discomfort. Colour too can be attractive to some and feel jarring to others. Consider when house-hunting and a room has been decorated bright red and purple: for some this will be exciting and stimulating, whereas someone else would feel over-whelmed and want to leave immediately. We need to remember that a child's vision is not just a process but involves all these aspects of 'seeing' with individual reactions to what may be in their environment.

A further aspect to thinking about colour is that there do appear to be some gender differences in its appreciation and perception. Boys and girls have anatomic differ-ences in the presence and distribution of cells sensitive to colour and those sensitive to location and motion (Sax, 2006). Girls appear to have more of the former and boys the latter, providing some insight into the generalized abilities of boys to be more spatially aware while girls are more aware of subtle differences in colour. 'Peach is a fruit not a colour' is the anguished cry from a 'round robin' by men on the Internet. However, when thinking about how boys and girls may be experiencing their surroundings, such differences may mean a great deal. For example, the female tendency to use lots of colours when drawing coupled with a mainly female workforce in the early years, may lead to such choices meeting with more approval than the orange, brown and grey chosen by the boys.

Hearing and communication

As in vision, hearing is not strictly utilitarian as it too, brings with it a range of psycho-logical properties. Being able to hear helps in the detection and location of sound; we also can detect its pitch and tone, whether we like it or not. Hearing enables us to use verbal communication with all of its power and variation, listen to and play music and have awareness of all the sounds that surround us. In other words, the ability to hear means that we give sounds meaning. How we hear is rather a magical mystery – much like our understanding of most of our senses, although perhaps the process of how we see is probably the best understood.

Given our understanding of the brain and how it works on electrical activity, sound waves too become 'translated' in electrical pulses which once mediated by the brain re-emerge into what we can identify specifically, such as a cat's miaow, a dog barking, the sound of a car backfiring, the voice of someone you know. Much of how the hearing mechanism actually works remains elusive but what is known is that sounds have features in common, such as intensity, frequency and location, and each of these is represented in a different way in the auditory neural pathways – again similar to the stimulus 'breakdown' in vision into components such as colour, form, motion and depth. Equally, like vision, there are overarching organizational principles dependent on the type of stimulus.

A difference, however, is that information from both ears is sent to both hemi-spheres, although most of the left ear's signals go to the right hemisphere and vice versa. Sound location is achieved by the brain 'comparing' the differences in timing and intensity between each ear; for example a sound on one side would reach the same side ear first and then the other ear a fraction later, and location would be based on these differences. A sound presented to the midline, however – and most parents talk to their baby looking directly at them – reaches the two ears more or less simultaneously, potentially providing a 'baseline' for the processing of sounds.

However, the midline does not give information about location other than in that modality, and so localizing sounds from elsewhere will depend on the baby's growing experience of listening to sounds from other directions. Familiarity with the sounds of the parents' voices, especially perhaps the mother's, will help this – as will probably the musicality of 'motherese' (discussed further in Chapter 3). This is the wonderful, sing-song way of speaking to babies that nearly all females, and some males, adopt. This type of talking also often involves lots of head movements, and this could be the beginning of helping to localize a sound other than in the midline.

We also have the capacity to hear our own voices, but with adaptations by the brain so that we don't deafen ourselves if we scream or cry. The auditory centres in the left and right hemispheres of the brain too echo the types of function of the language centres in each hemisphere of the brain.[16] The left hemisphere appears to be involved in the processing and perception of speech (Schiffman, 2001), while the right hemisphere 'predominates in the holistic and integrative processing and perception of spatial information as well as certain nonverbal sounds, including music' (p.363). These functions reflect the more analytical functions of the left hemisphere overall and the holistic nature of processing in the right hemisphere with its emotional overtones.

The brain also adapts sound in other ways, for example Budiansky (2003) points out that before the age of four months, human infants are confused by the echoes of sound; for example an initial sound coming from the right may 'bounce off' a wall or other large object to the left of the listener so that the sound is heard from another as well as the original direction. After four months of age, babies seem to be able to localize much better as the maturing brain circuits appear to 'actively suppress' the echo. The identification of different sounds has significance when this is linked by the finding that by eight months, babies all over the world have learned to discriminate the sounds of their own language and gradually lose their acute sensitivity to the sounds of languages they don't experience by about a year.

Babies around eight months have begun to localize sounds from behind but still have some difficulty locating sounds from above and below; gradually by around eighteen months the child will be able to localize sounds from different directions. Perceiving the distance of sounds is crucial: we need to be able to assess the sound of an approaching car, for example. In evolutionary terms, we need to be able to discern whether danger is near or far. Incidentally, the instinctive habit of cupping a hand around an ear in order to hear better does have real significance as pulling the earlobe (pinna) forward enables the earlobe to 'catch' more sound, and so a child who is noted to be doing this could be demonstrating that they are having difficulty hearing.

A further vital role for the ear, or rather the inner ear, is that of balance. Balance and posture depend on ongoing information from current body posture and movement, especially the head and eyes, and it must be remembered that eye position and head/ body position can be independent; for example we can look to the side without turning our head or body. The vestibular system is extremely complex but in its relevance to development, it illustrates that the infant's increasing head and body control over time allows this complex network to be put in place. Walking, for example, involves not only motor control but also posture and balance, and this complexity may be initiated by the baby first learning to focus on a face and attend to a voice which allows for both attention to direction and location of sound to be initially experienced.

Smell and taste

Like vision, hearing and information from the position and sensation from the body, smell and taste provide the infant with information about their world. Smell, incidentally, is the one sense which transmits straight into the brain, bypassing the usual thalamic relay station, and unsurprisingly has strong connections with taste, emotional and memory processes in the brain.

Babies are born with a sense of smell and can identify within a few hours their mother's breast milk compared to that of others', and we have already noted that babies are also born with the ability discern different tastes. From around six months of age, many babies are gradually introduced to different textures and flavours through the process of 'weaning' and as Robinson (2003) describes, babies have to 'learn' how to swallow something thicker than liquid which provides links between physiology and emergence of skills. Synchronizing swallowing with food intake rehearses not only eating skills but also different jaw and tongue movements, which may also serve to provide the muscular framework for language. Lip movements that support blowing bubbles or 'raspberries' also support different lip movements for language, and babies – as well as babbling and shrieking – also frequently practice these blowing skills with huge enjoyment, demonstrating once again the close links that all aspects of development often have with one another.

Smell and taste are also the two senses most obviously involved with the primary needs: hunger, thirst and later, as adults, sexual activity. Smell and taste also warn humans of danger. Humans, including human infants, have a strong sensation of 'disgust' to unpleasant smells and tastes, which would seem to have an evolutionary purpose as such reaction is often evoked by what would be truly dangerous, such as poisons or rotting substances. This evolutionary safeguard and the associations with our most fundamental needs also mean that there are very strong emotional overtones to the experiences of these senses. We are all aware, for example, of the profound emotional impact of eating disorders, and even when someone appears to refuse or dislike something we have cooked this can evoke very powerful feelings of rejection as for some, to offer and give food is a sign of love and affection. The social aspects of eating are also very deep-seated in many cultures, forming part of traditional ways of hospitality, of friendship, and have a place in many religious rituals and traditions. Eating together has a strong symbolic component, and the apparent loss in many families of this simple act has often been cited as contributing to a deterioration in general well-being as 'togetherness' becomes diminished.

Smell too has links with emotional well-being. For example, research by Cupchik et al. (2005) found a strong association between the types of recall of positive reading matter when associated with a pleasant smell, and the reading of negative subject matter associated with an unpleasant smell. The finding was that the combination of the two positives resulted in more accurate recall of character details, while the negative/negative resulted in a more accurate recall of settings. Schiffman (2001) also notes some research which shows that if an 'unfamiliar neutral odour – even a very low intensity' was associated with a stressful emotional event, experience of the odour at a later date produced 'appropriate mood and attitudinal changes'.

This raises some interesting possibilities when considering how infants and young children lay down their sensory memories of their experiences and relationships. For example, adults may be particularly fond of a particular soap or perfume and this scent will become part of their personality that is experienced by others. A child may come to associate a scent with a memory of the particular adult *and* the experiences associated with that relationship. In addition, the smell of the setting when first encountered can contribute to the child's total experience of their first day, influencing their emotional responses.

As well as this deep association, we have to remember that in a more transient way, a scent or aroma may be pleasing or distasteful and that we all tend to have our particular likes and dislikes of various smells and tastes. An interesting exercise could be simply to ask friends and colleagues their favourite and most disliked smell and taste. Favourites can range from vanilla and rose to tar and seaweed – and for many very young children, poo has fascination! Memories too, often of childhood experiences, can be evoked simply by thinking of what these smells and tastes might be as associations are conjured up through the reality of these likes and dislikes.

In addition, as anyone who has had a cold will testify, taste is influenced by the ability to smell food or drink and the loss of one's sense of smell can lead to food tasting bland and uninteresting. However, even here, individual likes and dislikes and sensitivities to tastes are important. Cultural influences on the types of food that a child may be accustomed too will influence a child's reactions to what is given to them as well as their particular preferences to taste, smell, texture and colour – many children go through a phase of liking food of a particular colour. Sensitivity and awareness of such responses is helpful when supporting children with their dietary needs. This does not mean that children become tyrants and dictate the dietary needs of the whole household, but it does mean that some leeway can be afforded to a child's genuine dislike of some textures in food and smells.

The essential nature of movement

The senses and awareness of movement and the ability to position ourselves in space constitutes a fundamental part of getting to know the body and finding out about the world. I have quoted from Sheets-Johnstone (1999) before (Robinson, 2008), but feel that this paragraph says the fundamentals about movement so beautifully:

> Fundamental facets of our knowledge of the world derive from our basic kinetic corporeal commonalities. As infants we all explored the world about

us. We picked up objects, put them in our mouths, turned them about in our hands, studied them from various perspectives. Through touch and movement we come to constitute the world epistemologically for ourselves; we came to know a spoon, a ball, an apple, a book, a box . . . from touching it and moving it directly and/or from moving ourselves in relation to it. Moving toward objects, approaching them from different directions, stopping in front of them, peering down or up at them, grasping them, mouthing them, we engaged the world on the basis of our tactile-kinesthetic bodies. . . . Coming to know the world in a quite literal sense means coming to grips with it.

(1999, p.226)

Movement, therefore, is integral to development both as a part of development and its role in the optimal development of other skills and abilities.

Most people are aware that babies are born with a set of reflexes and you will be familiar with the primary ones of rooting/sucking, stepping, startle and grasp, but Goddard (2005) mentions others such as the asymmetrical tonic reflex, which is when the baby turns its head to the side, the arm and leg on that side extend while the arm and leg on the other side bend.

These so-called 'primitive' reflexes in the newborn gradually blend or subsume into more conscious activity usually within the first six to eight months of life. This together with the emergence of other reflexes – in particular the 'postural reflexes' – point to a greater integration of communication between the hemispheres as the infant develops. This gradual shift between actions that are mainly 'reflexive' in nature to those that are more coordinated and purposeful is an essential part of development, and if these reflexes remain can lead to difficulties in later learning. Perhaps one of the most interesting facets regarding movement is that every movement requires both action and inhibition, i.e. the stretching of one muscle means the contraction of another. In fact, inhibition is a guiding principle in the human brain whereby in order to have organization and regulation of activity there has to be both excitatory impulses and inhibitors. It is interesting to consider that behaviour requires action and inhibition too, both at the observed physical level and in the psychology of the individual to make decisions and to restrict impulses.

When the child begins to be more mobile, movement involves posture, i.e. 'readiness to move', structure and function, as well as the neurophysiology of nerve centres in the brain. The first movements and play function as a 'training ground' for motor functions (Berthoz, 2000). The baby who can now sit steadily uses his body as the reference point, turning both head and body to look at something. Once the baby is mobile, links with the visual system come into play as the baby has to find other ways of keeping objects constant in space. Before eighteen months the infant will fix on a landmark, which is why placing an object for the child to reach supports crawling.

When finally walking, the baby uses additional strategies to keep objects in space constant while moving around the room – hence the bumping into objects which is not just a lack of physical coordination but also the work being done in the brain to 'update' the information from vision, motor movements, posture and purpose in moving. However, while the ambulant young child doesn't need to 'fix' on something to aim at, they (and we) still guide our direction of movement from where we are looking – so telling a child to 'look where you are going' is slightly wrong as the child is going where they are looking! The link between vision and control of posture is very strong in very young children, and their ability to remain upright can be influenced by what is around them. This means that any visual difficulty in children which may be undetected would then influence their ability to move around their surroundings and perhaps be labelled a 'clumsy' child.

Sometimes we may not appreciate just how much exquisite work is done by our brains in helping us stay upright and know where we are in space and in relation to other objects be around us. As Berthoz puts it – 'am I in my bed or hanging from the ceiling?' For babies and very young children this amazing coordination between muscles, joints, vision, balance takes time and practice. The almost instinctive need for many children to climb, clamber, swing in dizzying circles and/or upside down is a way of establishing these neural networks, as is the early movement of babies, reaching, crawling, standing and taking first steps. These activities also build on the information gained from being lifted, swung, laid down, jiggled, bounced and rocked in all the day-to-day activities of being a baby.

What Berthoz also emphasizes is that movement is pleasurable both in itself and in its achievement. It is doubtful if anyone would query the sense of joyous achievement that a baby appears to display when they first take a step – matched only by the joyous encouragement of parents. Babies too, simply in their reaching, must gain a certain sense of satisfaction or pleasure when they touch the face of their parent, feel the sensation of their food or grasp the favoured toy. When a little older, the joy felt in simply moving can be great, such as when a dance step is achieved or a somersault is successful. The current emphasis on exercise, which is mainly in response to alleviating the growing tendency for obesity, perhaps also needs to reaffirm just how pleasurable moving can be if allowed to be playful. It may be that it is the element of the joy of play that is really being lost for some children with all the subsequent potential lack in coordination and general motor skills.

There have also identified some gender differences in the development of motor skills. The way in which we develop control over our bodies starts with the head and neck and then the trunk – including, as McClure (2008) points out, the shoulders. When this growth is in place, the connections between the large limbs and the body become slowly established, and finally refinement of movement in the fingers and toes. Building up the large muscles helps these finer ones to grow and develop. Girls appear to develop these connections earlier than boys; McClure suggests this is because girls have more connections between the two hemispheres in the brain, which may indeed be the case. However, it is possible that there may also be an evolutionary 'throwback' with boys needing a longer preparation for these large muscles to develop, which may be the necessary foundation for the patterns of male muscle growth in adolescence. Girls, however, can carry out fine motor movements around this age with considerable success, including holding a pencil, threading and sticking.[17] Boys, however, at around four years are still developing their large muscles and need 'whole leg movement' for example. Therefore boys may find many of the fine motor activities particularly hard and so may become disruptive and negative in their attitude if the fine motor activities are seen as being of particular importance in any group setting – such as the ability to hold a pencil. Girls may be seen as more amenable and therefore probably praised, and the boys, rushing outside to construct or paint on walls with large brushes, may be seen as somehow 'lacking' in their motor skills while at the same time their technical skills may be unappreciated.

Such understanding of the differences between muscle development between boys and girls has very real implications for the types of activities, together with expectations and attitudes towards either gender in both family and group contexts. The difficulties many boys have in sitting still, their preference for being outside, not feeling the cold and desire for action may all provide situations in which these natural inclinations do not fit the particular environment; boys are therefore sometimes perceived as disruptive, difficult or 'hard to control'.

Summary

This chapter has set out to highlight the importance of understanding how our brains work with the particularly crucial role of early experience that sets down those fledgling neural pathways which subsequent experience can modify but never totally eradicate. The senses too, linked together by both experience and our emotional responses, are the gateway to finding out about ourselves and our environment.

The common existence of the senses and the overall architecture, structure and broad functions of the brain provides the common framework for all human beings but the environment, both psychological and physical, in which we find ourselves begins the real work of forming the individual we sense as 'me'. The highly individual nature of perception, the levels of sensory experience and the types of emotions that are most often aroused in us mean that there is a genuine reality in the Early Years Foundation Principle of the 'Unique Child'. We are all unique in sometimes subtle rather than florid ways, but these differences and those that may exist because of our particular gender mean that adults must be open to thinking about what the child might be sensing and feeling.

As said at the beginning, the behaviour of a child can be considered within a series of frameworks, including how sensitive or not they may be to the myriad stimuli around them and the levels of brain growth and maturation. The broadly time-related emergence of skills and abilities, growth and change, will be discussed in Chapter 4, but it is to the quality of interactions, relationships and emotional responses that we now turn.

Chapter 3

Interactions, relationships and emotional responses

This chapter considers the third of the key frameworks suggested to support the further understanding of children's behaviour. This is the magical but sometimes rocky road to how we learn to be the *type* of person we will become. Each baby is truly a unique individual with, most likely, an inborn temperament. However, how that temperament is modified or enhanced, how the child's capacities are encouraged or diminished, rests ultimately on the type of experiences the baby will encounter – especially and most importantly their early relationships. The feelings such relationships engender provides the bedrock on which not only the tenor of future relationships may be built, but also attitudes, motivation, feelings of self-worth and disposition towards learning. Therefore this chapter dwells at some length on these early interactions.

Thinking of development as a journey is undoubtedly something of a cliché but nevertheless, like many clichés and stereotypes, there is truth embedded within it. For the baby and young child, the beginning of this journey is one that they cannot travel alone but instead prepares them for eventually travelling their own individual pathway the best way they can. There is a beginning and end to life, birth and death, and how we learn to live the life we are gifted between these mysterious entrances and exits is set down in our early years. In some ways, this seems so obvious, and yet the reality of the prime importance of setting the scene for the child to become an adult has become fraught with anxiety and overladen with complexities regarding what those early years are for.

Many of us in the early years field see this time in life – when the child is at his or her most vulnerable – as the time for adults to lead the way. To shine a light for the child as they begin their journey to understanding and independence. To support them in learning about themselves as a separate, loved and unique individual who is then capable to live and love, play and work. In addition, what we hope is that this 'preparation time' allows for enough inner strength to gradually build so that the child understands that there is hope, that obstacles can be overcome and that loss, while painful in the extreme, can be borne and perhaps even greater strength eventually achieved.

However, what can happen in the early years is that adults may not be available for the child, emotionally and/or socially and/or physically, or that they imbue the child with their own dreams and desires, pain and distress along a spectrum of vanquished hopes. The adult's own particular view of the world – built of course on their own experiences – can cloud and distort the view they present to the child. Adults may prize academic success or see learning as futile, may see the child as an extension of themselves or as the means to their own happiness and self-esteem – a baby to love them, for example. Society too can place huge pressures on parents so that their capacity to think about their baby becomes muddled as they listen to the plethora of advice regarding how to deal with crying, feeding and holding. The very nature and value of nurturing may also be put under strain as mothers may be encouraged to return to work, even in circumstances when finances may not be an issue. However, what might it cost us as a society if we don't pause, take a breath and pay renewed attention to the devastating simplicity of the needs of children and consider the potential outcomes if these needs are not met?

In the beginning

In the previous chapter, there was a reference to Michelangelo's painting *The Creation of Adam*, in particular the space between the finger of God and that of Adam. This image seemed to reflect the space between the tendrils of the human brain cell, but it also reflects the space or state of separation between all human beings. In addition, just like the brain cell, there is a need for a method of communication which is both a bridge which spans the divide and a means for linking people together. What is remarkable is that the methods of communication between people influences the connectivity between our brain cells – so experience does indeed shape and influence the fine architecture of the brain, but it also represents something much deeper. We need to *connect* to other human beings in order to *develop* as a unique human being, and furthermore, this connection influences the shape of our personality, fine-tuning those aspects of our humanity which may be both experience expectant and experience dependent: 'A child must find human companions who will share meanings passionately' (Trevarthen, 2006).

Such connection, of course, does not start only when a baby is born. As a foetus, the baby is already contained by and connected to its mother, growing within her body and nurtured by a complex array of biological systems for its health and well-being. However, this growing being is not simply a 'passenger' waiting for the time to be born. Research has indicated that the foetus will respond to an amniocentesis needle as early as the first trimester (Sallenbach, 1993). Furthermore, some very early research has indicated that it will move in synchrony to a rhythm (Goodlin and Schmidt, 1972).

The unborn baby, however, is not just responsive to external stimuli but is, of course, profoundly influenced by the mental and physical well-being of the mother. Perhaps one of the most striking pieces of research demonstrating the impact of the mental health of the mother is that by Tiffany Field and her colleagues (2004). Her research of mothers with depression showed not only that foetal movements were slightly increased overall in these mothers, but also the actual *level* of movement appeared to vary with the *type* of depression. That is, mothers who later appeared to have a more 'intrusive' type of depression had babies who tended to be slightly less active than those whose mother's appeared to be more withdrawn later. In other words, these unborn babies appeared to be already adapting in some subtle way to the mental state of their mother, how she was actually *feeling* about herself and potentially about her child. This finding interestingly reflects studies indicating that stimulating music played to the foetus between twenty-two and twenty-eight weeks results in a *lowering* of heart rate (Lorch et al., 1994).[1] Such findings may indicate the complex interplay of what is optimal for the child at any particular developmental phase – including prenatally. It is possible that some experiences(even if apparently positive or fun) may be over-stimulating during a particular phase of development leading to physiological changes in the body's effort to reduce potentially raised stress levels, thereby influencing the child's behaviour.

Further research on the well-being of the mother during pregnancy include studies by Bergman et al. (2007), Talge et al. (2007) and O'Connor et al. (2002), and these indicate that prenatal stress appears to have long-term consequences on behaviour and attitudes to learning even when controlled for such things as birth weight, gestational age and delivery. The O'Connor study, for example, 'found strong and significant links between antenatal anxiety and children's behavioural/emotional problems at age 4 years.' The findings seem to remain significant even though there was potential bias as the findings were based on maternal report. However, it has to be said that findings in studies can vary, and the mechanisms as to how antenatal stress influences the emotional/behavioural world of the child postnatally are far from clear. Nevertheless, the intertwined and co-regulating dance of communication between mother and child after birth begins before birth, with the foetus impacting on the mother's body through hormonal influences, and maternal physiology also adapting and responding, embedded in a context of the mother's own mind and heart.

However, there is a bridge that spans the gap between the womb and the external world, and that is the voice of the mother. While the baby can potentially hear the voice of the father and any siblings, become acquainted with familiar sounds such as washing machines and television themes, it is this particular voice which will have the greatest resonance. Perhaps it is no coincidence that the unborn baby's hearing develops usually by the twenty-sixth week (Flohr, 2005). Edwards and Hodges (2007) also note that 'musical expressiveness and responsiveness appear at birth (even before birth) and, given appropriate learning opportunities and reinforcements, develop at a natural pace throughout childhood and into adulthood' (p.15).

The song of the mother (and father too)

'Motherese' or more prosaically 'Infant Directed Speech' (IDS) or 'parentese' are the names given to the type of pitch, tone and rhythm in the speech that mothers, and fathers to some extent, almost instinctively use when speaking to babies. Even young children can be heard talking to their infant siblings in such a tone (often at a very high pitch). The existence of this type of musical speech in mothers across cultures would seem to suggest its evolutionary importance and, together with the initial instinctive orientating of babies to faces, discussed below, provides the opportunity for a wealth of both sensory and emotional information impacting on a range of infant development.

For example, in reflecting on the relationship between mother and child, perhaps it is the sound of motherese, it's rhythmic tone and quality which not only helps bind together the baby's own sensory experiences but also acts to bind together the sight, sound, smell and emotional experience of the mother who is talking to him. So the baby experiences itself and also the holistic impression of this other person helping to ascertain who they are, i.e. this voice, this face, this feeling equals my mum whom I can recognize even before I know that she exists consistently in space and time.

While 'nature' appears to set the scene for the baby to get to know its mother through sensory and reflexive activity, nevertheless in order for the baby to 'grow' psychologically as well as physically, this beginning needs to shift into a more 'knowing' awareness of who is who. This awareness of a truly significant 'other' may also be supported by analyses of maternal speech to pre-verbal infants which reveals that individual mothers use only a limited set of tunes they adapt in different situations and perhaps most importantly still, the 'tunes of each mother differ from those of every other mother' (Flohr, 2005, p.26). Another highly speculative notion on my part regarding motherese comes from studies of song in birds (Llinas, 2002). If I have understood the studies correctly, it would seem that in many bird species it is the males that sing, while the females sing when there is hormonal input. All the necessary physical 'equipment' is present in the female birds, but it seems they need an external stimulus to find their voice. Because of the very particular nature of motherese, it is interesting to wonder whether it is the influence of the birth and the rush of oxytocin which accompanies it that helps its tone and rhythm to become established in the particularly unique way for each mother to her child.

Motherese may also support the growing coordination of movement in the baby as its tempo can activate the motor cortex, as has been demonstrated in adults who are listening to music. Rhythm, as Sachs (2007) points out, is an integration of sound and movement and when speaking to babies, mothers are rarely still. As they talk, their facial expression changes, heads bob up and down and their hands may move across the body of the infant in instinctive time to the rhythm they are using. Rhythm is also part of being able to 'keep time', which is essential for moving smoothly, and rhythm is also a pattern, and patterns are how the brain essentially organizes information. If we remember that the cerebellum is involved in timing of movements, perhaps these rhythms are impacting on and supporting the development of connections between this structure and those other parts of the brain involved in movement and body awareness as well as the emotional quality of face and voice. Trevarthen (2007a) describes microanalysis of the hand and body movements of a blind five-month old baby as she listens to her mother singing two songs, and the baby is noted to move her hands as if she was conducting the mother's singing. This understanding of tempo also ties in with research by Honing et al. (2009), which suggested that 'beat induction', i.e. the awareness of a regular pattern while listening to music, is active in both non-musicians and functional 'right after birth'.

Therefore, the earliest songlike speech of a mother to her baby potentially helps to organize movement, sensory and emotional information into an integrated experience. Detailed analysis of this type of speech in tandem with the sounds and movements of the baby shows a wondrous display of timing with pauses and bursts of vocal activity, accompanied too by the mother's facial expressions, eye gaze and hand/body movements. This vocal activity varies not only in rhythm but also in pitch and tempo with mother following baby's lead, adding some additional features of her own and then waiting for the baby's response and adjusting once more. In such situations, it is hardly surprising that this communication has been termed a 'dance'. Fathers too can communicate in this way, and Flohr and Trevarthen (2007) provide an example of a father and his premature baby matching one another's timing of vocalizations.

Motherese is, of course, all about communication in all its forms. Being talked to, watching mouth movements, their association with the accompanying sounds and localization of those sounds (initially from the midline) to support hearing also underpins the eventual production of speech in the baby. Links with our understanding of brain function also exist, as the left hemisphere has been noted to be more associated with the perception of rhythm and the right with the perception of pitch – which has an emotional content. If we recall Trevarthen's (2004) findings mentioned in Chapter 2 that the left hemisphere's language areas appeared to have some different formation to the right even at twenty-four weeks gestation, it may also be that not only are we 'primed' for language but that the rhythm of motherese provides further opportunity for the maturation of these areas. Incidentally, people with Alzheimer's disease are 'sometimes able to engage in musical activities long after other cognitive functions have been lost' (Edwards and Hodges, 2007), perhaps indicating the deep-seated nature of a sense of music or musicality[2] and its attractiveness to our ears both as babies and as adults.

A possible loss of knowledge of traditional lullabies may also lead to mothers and fathers not realizing how actual singing helps not only to calm babies but also to interest them and 'regulate their arousal level' (Flohr, 2005). Of course, babies and young children don't mind what parents sing or how they sing – just being sung to will probably be very pleasing to most of them. Babies also like being talked to but studies have indicated that babies are 'transfixed' by their mother's singing, with signs of prolonged visual attention and a stilling of body movement accompanied by a more sustained effect on the lowering of cortisol levels. So perhaps it is not just pleasure but something deeper that occurs when babies hear the song of the mother.

Lack of communication

Both the auditory and visual systems are maturing during early childhood, and while the auditory system develops earlier than the visual system (we hear better than we can see at birth),[3] it also develops more slowly to allow for fine discrimination of sounds which not only helps speech but also has a 'knock-on' effect for reading and writing. We can see, therefore, that initial reflexive activity of orientating to faces and the sensitivity to voice develops into a dynamic interplay between mother and baby, with resulting influences on emotions, movement and mind/body physiology based on their mutual communication. However, Braun and Bock (2007, p.34) sound a clear warning note for a *lack* of communication, noting that:

we can only imitate sounds that we can acoustically identify with high precision and even more importantly only the continuous feedback by critically listening to our own voice will perfect our speech skills.

They go onto say that 'if the acquisition of language is incomplete due to inappropriate stimulation' instead of *'individual* and *interactive* communications with caregivers' (my emphasis), children are highly likely not only to have speech difficulties but also difficulties in reading. In particular, they cite children whose main auditory experience is via television or videos 'which are way too fast for the juvenile brain'.

If we remember the dominance of the right hemisphere in the first eighteen months to two years, its strong parallel maturation with the formation of attachment, links with self-awareness and emotional processing, we can also link this information with the fact that both mothers and babies appear to have a way of communicating which is intrinsically attractive to both. The fact that we hear so well at birth and that this method of communication allows for easier understanding of sounds, accompanying emotional content and facial expression suggests that motherese is a powerful and *necessary* part of the communication repertoire of parent to baby.

Therefore, as Braun and Bock have indicated, the *lack* of such communication and all its associations for a baby because of parental neglect and/or communication which is mainly suffused with sadness, anger or hostility may produce patterns of experience with potentially profound impact on the deepest, most receptive and perhaps ultimately least flexible parts of the human brain. Trevarthen (2007), in his extensive studies of the rhythmic communication between babies and their parents, notes that in both mother and baby, loss of the ability to be literally 'in tune' with one another can lead to discordance. For example, an unwell and/or premature baby is often hard to understand as their responses may be out of kilter with the mother's approaches, while a sad or depressed mother appears to find it much harder to communicate with their baby in the singing patterns of motherese.

This suggests that it is the matching of sounds, movements and expressiveness between mother and baby which help support development in a range of domains, not least the infant's emerging understanding of safety and trust embedded in these loving exchanges. It is important to recognize that these episodes of close communication can be relatively brief,[4] but nature has provided wonderful opportunities for interactions/communication to take place, such as when feeding, changing a nappy, bathing or settling a child to sleep. Dr Ed Tronick, in his video presentation of the 'still face procedure' to be discussed below, notes that it is only about '20–30% of the time' that child and parent are totally 'in synch'. It is more usual to be moving in and out of these communicative dances. What seems to be important is that the 'in synch' does happen and that mismatches can be 'repaired'.

I witnessed a powerful example of this on a video recording of a mother and baby having a wonderful 'conversation'. Suddenly, the mother leaned forward and kissed the baby on the forehead. We observers were as startled as the baby appeared to be! However, mother seemed to realize that she had mistimed her kiss and gave the baby time to recover, noting the baby's turn away, and then once baby looked back she slowly appeared to almost 'reintroduce' herself, and resumed play only when she could see baby was ready. The 'repair' interaction was seconds only and provided evidence of the speed in which we can process facial expressions. Cavanagh (2005) noted how the speed of emotional expression and response in infants has been demonstrated by Beatrice Beebe[5] through freeze-frame video recording and other research has indicated that the actual processing speed of facial processing is emotions first, then recognition of a face and then whose face. In other words, what we sense as the *emotion* on a face is what is going to have the main impact. This example also provides an illustration of how awareness of another's feelings/responses influences how we adjust and adapt our own behaviour.

Food for thought

We can now make some links as to how a lack of such communication might influence a child's behaviour, including their motivation and attitudes towards themselves and others. Jaffe et al. (2001) notes that the quality of the interaction between a mother and young baby can potentially indicate the quality of attachment relationship months later, so these early exchanges have a profound effect on the child's early foundations of their emotional health and well-being.

If a child has not had the opportunities from birth for such 'individual and interactive communication', as Braun and Bock (2007) indicated this may influence their capacity to relate to both their peers and other adults If we also think through all the other effects of talking to or not talking to the baby and young child, we can see a range of potential difficulties which may arise. For example, if we think of the possible effect on muscle coordination, a lack of early interaction could result in a slight 'clumsiness' and lack of coordination, with long-term effects on the ability to read and write.

In recent years there has been a growing recognition of the importance of early communication between parents and children, and this has led to the establishment of a range of interventions to encourage such communication, and ultimately literacy, such as those initiated by the National Literacy Trust and the Primary National Literacy Strategy (England) with their emphasis on supporting parents reading to and communicating with their babies and very young children. Local initiatives that involve and encourage parents to read and sing to their children also indicate widespread recognition of the importance of such communication. Furthermore, research by Zeedyk (2008c) on baby and toddler experiences when in a buggy found that those children in forward facing (i.e. away from the parent) had far lower levels of communication than those in the more traditional prams/buggies which faced towards the parent. As children can spend significant amounts of time in a buggy whrn parents go visiting, shopping and so on, the opportunity to simply chat to the baby is once again lost. For the child too, it is very difficult to make contact with the parent to express excitement, discomfort or any kind of distress.

Ultimately, it seems evident that a lack of warm and loving communication can send a long shadow across the growing image of the child's self-worth, self-esteem, aptitudes and motivation – and thereby behaviour.

The voice of the baby – the separation call

The first sound a baby makes tends to be a cry. In fact, years ago newborn babies were often made to cry by having their bottoms gently smacked as this encouraged a deep breath allowing the lungs to expand. This rude awakening to life outside the womb is not carried out any more but nevertheless the cry remains the initial and long-lasting call of the baby to its mother. It is a sound too that the mother will find difficult to ignore and also, over time, she will be able to identify variations in the cry, such as if the baby is hungry rather than cold or wet as the hunger cry in particular appears to have a definite tone.

However, whatever the basic cause for the discomfort, the cry serves a profound purpose and is an evolutionary safeguard against potential danger, and any uncomfortable/painful feeling is going to feel dangerous to the baby. This type of 'calling' is shared by many other species; for example, Sunderland (2006) notes that if a puppy is taken away from its mother, it can cry as much as 700 times in 15 minutes. This highlights the fearfulness of isolation and separation from the sense of security and safety that the vast majority of young animals appear to experience when away from their mothers. Human babies too, from the moment of birth are away from the confines of the womb into a world that suddenly has no boundaries. They are totally helpless and vulnerable. Perhaps it is unsurprising that the instinctive reaction of mothers is to touch and hold their babies, keeping them closely to their bodies.

Christensson et al. (1994) studied the cry of babies in different care situations and found that human babies did recognize physical separation from their mothers and started to cry 'in pulses'. They also felt that this crying was not dependent on 'earlier social experience and may be a genetically encoded reaction to separation.' Again, this provides a powerful indicator for the need for closeness and connection, which in optimal circumstances will occur soon after birth. Some separations after birth are unavoidable because of problems in either mother or baby after the birth, but increasingly efforts are made to ensure that some form of contact between parents and their babies occurs in these circumstances through opportunities for touch and talking to the baby. For such babies and their mothers, their relationships can be re-established and grow once they are able to be together again. The plasticity/elasticity of the brain in the earliest years allows for change, meaning that babies and very young children can adapt to changing qualities in relationships and situations, although transitions – emotional as well as physical – will always take time.

For the *neglected* baby, there begins a developmental journey where all the necessary and ordinary day-to-day nurture is mainly denied, with possible consequences for emotional health (if no interventions) and potentially impacting on language development, motor control and understanding of their own self-worth. It is also worth considering the long-term effects on the well-being of those babies whose parents follow rigid regimes of contact, feeding and interaction, where babies are left to cry for no reason except that the child 'has to learn' to cope. Babies cry for a multitude of reasons, and if we recall that the amygdala is fully 'on line' at birth and is a prime detector for potential threat, we can wonder what such a lack of comforting can feel like. If we think back to the puppy and its persistent cries for its mother on separation, the lack of comfort given to a baby in such a situation may also be equally devastating. Sunderland (2006) notes that crying usually peaks when the 'baby is 3–6 weeks old and then abates at around 12 to 16 weeks'.[6]

It is possible that once the most basic of physiological rhythms outside the womb are slowly being established, i.e. feeding, sleeping, breathing patterns and heart rate, then the focus turns to ensuring that the baby experiences comfort to their distress whatever the cause. Repetition of experience allows the early 'wiring' between sensory and emotional experience.

Panksepp (1998), in his comprehensive studies of brain function and emotion, considers that there are various circuits in the brain which link to primary emotional experiences, including seeking, panic, rage, fear, with their allied neurochemical activity. The role of neurotransmitters was mentioned briefly in Chapter 2, and those such as oxytocin, opiods, serotonin, dopamine and cortisol are linked to how experiences are emotionally 'loaded' for the child. Warmth, soothing touch, a low voice, all increase levels of oxytocin and opiods – the brain's own intrinsic pain relief. In other words, the nurturing behaviour of the mother, whose own brain circuits, as suggested by Panksepp, appear to be more in tune with infant needs that a male brain, affects chemical, hormonal and other physiological changes in the human baby. Cacioppo and Patrick (2008, p.67) note:

> Signals that the senses receive from the environment trigger changes in the concentration and flow of these hormones and neurotransmitters. These chemicals serve as internal messages to prompt specific behaviour and this is when the genetic instructions at long last appear as individual differences in levels of anxiety or agreeableness or sensitivity to feelings of social isolation.

In other words, babies are individuals who will respond in varying ways to the complexities of their experiences. Nevertheless, the cry of the baby is a call for nurturing and comfort and the *reality* of the response from the beginning will influence those neurological pathways for good or ill. The building blocks of self-esteem and self-worth are laid down early indeed.

The importance of faces

As we have seen, the human baby is primed to communicate and to get to know their mothers right from the moment of birth. We have already noted the importance of the mother's voice, and its very attractiveness may help the baby locate the face which is going to be imbued with so much emotional information. This idea is potentially supported by research recently reported by the National Science Foundation.[7] This research found that musicians were more effective communicating in noisy environments, i.e. they could attend to a particular sound better than non-musicians. The researchers also pointed out that for most of us, hearing in a noisy room is hard for everyone but music training appears to help hear better. The implication was that music training could help children and adults who perhaps had learning and speech problems. However, we could also make a link between the effectiveness of motherese as a universal medium for speech to babies and how its tones may help the earliest discrimination of sounds within a language. This also provides further reflection on how the lack of early communication may have long-term impact.

The initial familiarity of sound is linked with the instinctive holding, touching and smelling of the baby by the mother, providing a range of sensory experience for both her and the baby that allows for the relationship to fully begin, with the focus now on the way in which both parent and baby spend time looking at one another, and what they will see will be emotional expressiveness both in the eyes and on the face.

What we understand by the expression on someone's face elicits a response in all of us, and such a reaction seems profoundly deep-rooted within our psyche. Babies are aware of differences in facial expression very early on in life and the importance of that expressiveness potentially lies in the cross-cultural existence of a series of basic expressions that seem to be common to all. These are: happy, sad, fearful, angry, surprise and disgust. Paul Ekman has spent much of his life's work studying the universality of these expressions and his studies indicate that people from a range of diverse cultures can recognize similar configurations in the face, for example smile, frown and so on, as denoting specific feelings (2004; Ekman and Davidson, 1994). Variations exist as to the context or reason for such expressions as these will be based on their particular culture/environment, but the facial expression is recognized as relating to a specific feeling. This suggests that there is a basic, universal language via facial expression (and indeed some gestures such as rubbing the tummy) which seems to be fundamentally understood and therefore allows for connection between humans no matter where they happen to be.

While the expressions on a baby's face may be more diffuse, i.e. a cry face may indicate sadness but also a degree of crossness, there is little doubt at the meaning of a smile and this then usually prompts more interaction between parent and baby – although as we have seen above, it is the cry and distressed face that initially is the call for nurture. The fundamental importance of the particular configuration of face muscles that allow the formation of these expressions is indicated by the way in which facial muscles are the only muscles that connect directly to the skin. Facial expressions are also influenced by the activity of the limbic system as facial muscles contract in precise configurations, indicating a particular expression in response to our situation.

From the moment of birth, research tends to indicate a preference for the mother's face. In fact as Cozolino (2006) points out, the 'fixation on the mother's face is an obligatory brainstem reflex that ensures the imprinting of this vital social information' (p.154). As we know already, the brainstem is fully developed at birth and the existence of this 'reflex' fixation means that the baby – once he has located the face – has a 'kick-start' in getting to know the person who is going to be, most probably, their main carer.

The human eye also – uniquely amongst other animals – shows the 'white', which also allows the direction of gaze to be more easily observed. We can refer back to the interesting phenomenon mentioned in Chapter 2 of 'sticky fixation'. If you recall, this means that it is relatively difficult for the baby to 'break its gaze' to look at the periphery if something comes into view. The intriguing outcome is that babies are supported in their direct looking at the face(s) of their parents through this facet of visual development. After about three months, the baby is more able to move its gaze, which allows the baby to become more aware of what is going on around them and to have more control over communication through being able to turn both head and eyes away when things get 'too much'.

The face of the baby, too, invites care and nurture. The size of the eyes in comparison to the face allows the gaze of the baby to be more prominent, and this in turn provokes and promotes long looking by the mother towards her baby. However, research has also indicated that again, the baby is no passive partner in these exchanges, as Messinger (2002) points out. He notes that the *intensity* of a baby's smile or sad face can also influence the type of response from the parent. Babies as early as ten months can also demonstrate different smiles for mother and an approaching stranger.

Studies by Strathearn et al. (2008), which examined maternal brain activity in response to a baby's cues, demonstrated that first-time mothers had activation in extensive brain circuits when looking at their own infant's face, and the *happy* face of their baby also impacted on the 'reward' circuitry in their brains.[8]

Babies and young children also monitor the facial expression of their parents constantly – not just when they are feeling anxious or unsure. Ed Tronick's work mentioned earlier developed a procedure known as the 'still face' experiment back in 1978 and repeated by him and many other researchers over the years. This is where mothers and their babies were involved first in face-to-face interactions and then the mothers were told to have a 'still face'. In babies from six months to children of two years and older, the response is telling. Babies and children are upset at this change in the interaction and try to attract the attention of the parent back to them. If the 'still face' is held for a few moments, the child becomes more agitated but can then simply give up trying to re-establish contact. Once the relationship is re-established, it can take a few moments for the children to feel comfortable again.

Interestingly, babies of depressed mothers appear to be less distressed by this procedure, and it is possible that they are more 'used' to a passive face. It is notable that six-month-old baby boys have been found to have more difficulty than girls in 'maintaining affective regulation' during the procedure (Tronick, 2007). In other words, they probably 'fell apart' more. Dr Berry Brazelton (in Karr-Morse and Wiley, 1997) also noted that the response to distress in boys appears to differ from that of girls. The girls in Berry Brazelton's still face studies tended to 'withdraw', while the boys 'become violent in their efforts to reengage their mothers' (pp.211–212). This difference in behaviour has links with the findings on late antenatal stress by O'Connor et al. (2002) alluded to earlier in this chapter. The behaviour of the boys reflected animal studies of late maternal stress antenatally, in that the boys showed inattention and/or hyperactivity. The tendency of boys to externalize their inner distress in such a manner does seem to predispose them to being seen as challenging and disruptive.

The emotional vulnerability of boys in the early years is often alluded to but somehow seems to get lost when thinking about the particular needs of babies and children. For example, the Green et al. report (2004), commissioned by the Department of Health and Scottish Executive, stated one in ten children and young people aged five to sixteen had a clinically diagnosed mental disorder (which also could suggest distress in the child much earlier than the formal diagnosis). It was also noted that 'boys were more likely than girls to have a mental disorder' (the ratio being 11 per cent and 8 per cent respectively), and boys were more likely to be diagnosed with a conduct disorder than girls (8 per cent compared to 4 per cent), but were said to be less likely than girls – although only marginally so – to have an 'emotional disorder' (3 per cent as opposed to 4 per cent). It could be argued that 'conduct disorder' *is* an emotional disorder if we think about the response of boys to the still face. Their feelings are potentially just as 'disordered' as that of the girls – the difference lies in how they *express* that distress.

The significance of the 'still face' experiment is that it not only indicates just how closely a baby can monitor the parent's face, but also the exquisite sensitivity to a change in expression. Lewis et al. (2000) asked the question why such sensitivity in a baby who is not able to 'stand up on his own for another six months'? The answer potentially lies in the limbic brain, discussed in Chapter 2. We appear to be able, from a very early age, to detect *emotionality* in others. We are just as primed by nature to be aware of someone else's emotional states as we are to hear a sound or feel a touch. For the baby and very young child, the guide to their own feelings and emotions is by monitoring the reactions of the parent to them. As Lewis puts it, 'emotional experiences begin as a derivative; a child gets his first taste of his feelings secondhand' (p.156), and so the understanding and insight into the child's feelings, the responses to their cries and later smiles, the interpretation of their needs, provides the bedrock for the child's understanding and awareness of their *own* feelings. Without this sound beginning, the child will grow not only to be less able to understand their feelings but also those of others. We cannot become attuned to someone else if we have not had the experience of someone being attuned to us.

Food for thought

Overall, the implication is that frequent and lasting face-to-face communication in early life is important for our emotional and social development, and this aspect of our development stays with us throughout our lifespan as we continue to use the length and type of gaze to indicate how we feel. Not being able to 'look someone in the eye' is often associated with feelings of guilt and/or shame, and we can also gaze 'longingly' at someone or something we desire. People who are first 'in love' often lock gazes at moments of high emotional intensity – reflecting those first weeks when mother and baby (and father too) are establishing the first bonds of love between them. Gaze is an inherent part of our social signalling to others of our emotional state, and while care must be taken regarding cultural and social differences in the way eye gaze is used, there is nevertheless something fundamental about being able to look at someone and share a moment of communication.

Problems with understanding facial expressions can therefore potentially disadvantage a child in their relationships with others. The problems of children with autism in their difficulties in accessing social information, including via facial expressions and eye gaze, is well documented. However, it is not only children who may have some neurological deficit affecting their ability to process facial expressions (and indeed faces per se). Children who have lacked opportunities for this intense face-to-face interaction with their parents also can have difficulties interpreting facial expressions. For example, children from abusive backgrounds can misinterpret a sad or fearful face for an angry one. In addition, they may have received a distorted view of themselves through mainly hostile and/or neglectful interactions.

Such a lack of early, nurturing care influences the child's whole response to their experiences. As Perry (2006) says, 'a neglected maltreated child is all too often an infant emotionally' (p.46).[9] Chronological age can sometimes be mistaken for the age at which a child may actually be functioning, when in reality such children may behave, react, respond in ways that reflect their early lack of nurture. Perry goes on to say that such children often do well 'one-to-one', much to the surprise of teachers and others. In fact, this type of interaction is providing them with a flavour of the intensive 'one-to-one' action that they probably lacked much earlier in life.

What we have to remember is that the quality of the relationship between parent and child is built on the *adult's* ability to be able to connect to the child, and this will influence not only the quality of the child's attachment relationship but also the way in which the child can then go out into the wider world and deal with it. This emotional connection is built on the simplest of things – talking, touching, looking, playing, all embedded in care and nurture opportunities that provide the 'neural footprints' for the child's journey through life.

However, there is a further magical implement that nature has provided to support the establishment of these early relationships, and that is imitation, to which we now turn.

Imitating me, imitating you

Imitation as a facet of human interaction has been known for centuries. More recently, Piaget (1959/2002) in particular was deeply interested in imitation but tended to comment mainly on object imitations witnessed during his extensive observations of his children. Put very simply, he saw imitation has having a 'cognitive' origin. Kugiumutzakis et al. (2005) provide a highly succinct review of Piaget's approach and how it influenced the way imitation was thought about for many years. However, over the past thirty or so years there has been a sea change in how imitation has been perceived and its role in development and interactions/relationships.

In particular it has been through the work of researchers studying infant imitation, combined with the discovery in Italy of 'mirror neurons' (Rizzolatti et al, 1995, 2002; Meltzoff and Prinz, 2002; Iacoboni, 2008), that the debate regarding the power, purpose and meaning of the ability to imitate has been extensive, comprehensive and intense, especially in determining whether the ability of newborns to imitate is 'true' imitation or not.

Mirror neurons themselves were originally identified in primates.[10] They are cells in particular locations of the brain that become activated when observation is made of grasping, placing and manipulating objects *as if the observer was also doing the action.* Brain imaging techniques have indicated that these cells also exist in humans, further indicating that humans too can 'mentally simulate another's actions' (Ramachandran and Oberman, 2006). This suggests that there is a physiological mechanism within us that forms a neural connection between the movement of the self and of another. The capacity to 'mentally' imitate someone's grasping and manipulating objects may also influence and support our gradual development of accurately reaching and grasping a variety of objects. After all, the ability to accurately reach and grasp a cup of coffee will be influenced by a variety of factors, such as the width of the handle, the delicacy of the cup or robustness of a mug, whether it is full or half full, piping hot or lukewarm – all subtly altering the way in which we will pick up our coffee and, of course, put it to our lips.

If we already have neural 'imitators' which have formed representations of where our mouth is by watching others move their hands to their mouths, this will help us in our first forays into self-feeding. Further research has provided intriguing speculation regarding the role of mirror neurons in the development of a deeper understanding of self and empathy with others, as mirror neurons have been found in parts of the brain that are involved in processing emotions and have also been discovered firing when seeing someone else in pain.

Because of these discoveries, mirror neurons have been suggested to play a part in the earliest manifestations of imitation. Babies have been found to imitate mouth opening and tongue protrusion only hours after birth[11] – something that baby chimpanzees also do (Cacioppo, 2008). The growing sense among researchers is that, while the existence of active mirror neurons in the infant brain is still speculative, imitation may be innate and also part of the repertoire that infants have in order to establish basic neural pathways which contribute both to the development of movement and to the communication pathways between baby and parent.

Zeedyk (2008a) provides an overview of those behaviours that have been 'tentatively attributed to mirror neurons' and these include: 'yawning, empathic identification with another's emotions, the spontaneous copying observed in children's play, the developmental imperative to acquire language' (p.10). Cacioppo (2008) also notes how the power of imitation provides a sense of synchrony and connection between people including if someone is uncertain, they will copy the actions of those around them – you may have had the experience of watching what implement someone is using for an unfamiliar dish, or following a crowd of people in order to find the exit from a department store or theatre. People who are emotionally very close also continue to unconsciously mirror one another's postures, and studies show that we tend to feel more comfortable when we have unconsciously experienced being imitated. In addition, Ramachandran and Oberman (2006) believe that dysfunctional mirror neurons may play a part in the genesis of autism. A purely personal speculative view is that mirror neurons 'need' face-to-face contact in order to become fully active and therefore, if they are implicated in the range of developmental areas indicated above, this could also add to the 'knock-on' effect we have already discussed for those children who have not had these regular experiences.

What is significant – whatever the aetiology of the ability to imitate – is that babies can and do imitate when only hours old. They also stop doing this kind of facial imitation (the same as baby chimpanzees) at around the same time, i.e. two to three months. Thus, as Cacioppo (2008) suggests, they stop when they are able to 'move onto the next stage of interaction – the ability to spontaneously smile and vocalize at other people.' So it would appear that their ability to imitate these facial actions corresponds with the time when babies are in a state of 'sticky fixation' and long-looking at parents, especially mothers, and ceases at about the same time that babies are able to look more easily in other directions.

However, even at six weeks, some babies can use imitation as a means of sorting out who people are by remembering and repeating an action seen the previous day (Meltzoff, 2002b). Later children use imitation of each other in play, and throughout the lifespan we unconsciously imitate the verbal language, gestures and body language of those to whom we feel close. Parents, of course, also imitate their babies and it appears that within the first eight months the 'flow' of imitation tends to be of the parent imitating the baby. After eight months, the flow reverses slightly and babies begin to imitate the actions of their parents and it is during this phase that communicative gestures begin to appear, such as waving 'bye 'bye or raising the arms to be picked up – something to be discussed further in Chapter 4 in the context of parents adjusting to developmental change. However, early imitation of the child's facial expressions is part of the interaction between parent and baby taking its place in that monitoring and mirroring of expression to help support interpretation and responses. If we link this with the findings by Nagy (2008) that newborn babies respond to the 'still face' procedure mentioned above, we can see that the capacity for imitation, plus the baby's responses to an inactive face as well as to the type of expression, provides strong indications for the need of active interactions to establish relationships in a profound way.

The potentially innate nature of imitation and its power to establish feelings of closeness and togetherness between adults, between adults and children, and between children themselves, has also lent itself to establishing contact with people who are withdrawn and uncommunicative for a range of reasons. Zeedyk (2008a) and Caldwell and Horwood (2008) movingly describe how social interaction is developed in people with such communicative impairments. Caldwell, for example, works with people with profound autism, and the particular methodology she has developed is termed 'intensive interaction and sensory integration'. It is interesting that the process entwines interaction and sensory experience – just as it is intertwined in the growing baby. The heart of the interaction is to use imitation of actions, gestures and vocalization as a 'gateway' to communication – again reflecting the mother's[12] interactions with her baby. O'Neill et al. (2008) note that 'joining in another person's behaviour both reduces stress and acts as a personal code' (p.59). They go on to say (p.61) that:

> the very act of observing and joining in with another person's behaviours encourages us to 'step back' and reduce the speed of our communication,

thus creating space for the shared (and perhaps unpredicted) communicative response to emerge.

Initiatives based on this intensive interaction with imitation as its base have been used in people with dementia, profound learning disabilities, institutionalized children, with congenitally deaf-blind people (using touch as the medium)[13] as well as those on the autistic spectrum, and a breakthrough in the adult or child's ability to communicate and be aware of the other has been achieved in the studies described. If Ramachandran and Oberon's speculation referred to earlier has validity, it could be that the intensive, delicate and sensitive imitation of these withdrawn people allows inactive and/or dysfunctional mirror neurons to become 'on line'. Again, it may also be that this type of interaction replicates to some extent the profound nature of the connectivity of these first exchanges between the mother and her baby.

Imitation, therefore, is not simply a 'cognitive' process but one which, potentially underpinned by neurologically primed innate and then conscious actions, plays a crucial part in the vital and necessary emotional and sensory communication between parent and child.

The story continues

So far in this chapter, the importance of very early communication within the baby's relationship with their parent has been discussed, with the potential implications of a lack of such interaction being indicated. However, the 'neural footprint' which is being laid down in these early weeks and months, forming the foundation for the child's growing sense of self, is tied in with the effects of general nurture and care which also impacts on the quality of the attachment relationship. The latter, too, while certainly not set in stone, also provides the template for future relationships.

The strength of these patterns and how they can impact on a child's later development and thereby behaviour is because they are occurring when the brain is growing at its fastest rate. Moment by moment, the connections between brain cells are being made, and eventually unwanted connections will wither or be pruned away (see Chapter 2). However, even within this early exuberance of brain growth and massive connectivity, the brain still identifies patterns within experiences. Just as the brain identifies patterns for motor activities such as walking, reaching and grasping, how we hold a pencil, how we move, dance, stand, play an instrument and so on, so emotional patterns are identified and laid down too (Llinas, 2002).

Lewis et al. (2000) describe it beautifully: they say that the brain 'changes a stream of incoming information into silently evolving neural structures.' They go on to add that 'formative experiences lay down resilient patterns that prevail for a lifetime.' These form the first 'footprints', and like footprints placed in cement, may fade but never quite disappear.

Another essential part of the child's formative experiences is the quality of their attachment relationship to their parents, and it is to this process that we now turn.

Attachment security – a defence against danger

The theory of attachment and its significance for the emotional life of all of us was developed by John Bowlby and has been studied, researched and investigated extensively since Bowlby first put forward his hypothesis for the essential nature of the child's 'tie' to his mother. Perhaps it is more accurate to say that while the emphasis was on the biological mother, Bowlby also recognized the child's attachment relationships to significant others, including the father, and that the essential component was the child's experience of being 'mothered'. Schofield and Beek (2007, p.10) have identified two particularly pertinent quotes from Bowlby's early works which led eventually to his seminal writings on attachment, separation and loss (1969, 1973, 1980, 1988):

> What is believed to be essential for mental health is that an infant and young child should experience a warm, intimate and continuous relationship with his mother (or permanent mother substitute – one person who steadily 'mothers' him) in which both find satisfaction and enjoyment.
>
> (Bowlby, 1953, p.13)

> Children are not slates from which the past can be rubbed by a duster or sponge, but human beings who carry their previous experiences with them and whose behaviour in the present is profoundly affected by what has gone before.
>
> (Bowlby, 1951, p.114)

These two quotes provide a succinct insight into the nature of attachment and its impact on later life. Bowlby was influenced in his work through both his own studies and his open-minded approach to research into animal behaviour. A particular influence was research on 'imprinting' by Konrad Lorenz and his famous studies into the behaviour of goslings. Bowlby began to pull together these findings hypothesizing that as babies, we humans – just as in other species – have an *instinctive* need to form a bond with our mothers for safety and security. His work met with a great deal of scepticism and downright hostility from his psychoanalytically minded colleagues. He also had to battle against what Lewis et al. (2000) call the 'iron grip of behaviourism' where the approach to child care was one of ignoring distress and minimizing contact.[14]

Bowlby's hypothesis, however, was supported by the research carried out by Harry Harlow and his sad, orphaned monkeys. Harlow's distressing work identified the needs of these baby monkeys above and beyond the need for food. In fact, the behaviour of these animals and the way they clung to a cloth-covered structure whenever possible and only went to a wire structure with a feeding bottle when necessary provided painful but unequivocal evidence of the need for warm, comforting touch. In human babies, the same needs are observed and, as we have already seen, nature has put in several factors that enable the relationship to begin. This evolutionary push for contact means that the baby will demonstrate behaviour that ensures the mother keeps close, which initially is crying, then smiling, reaching, vocalizing and once mobile will follow or run towards the mother for reassurance. I am sure we all have witnessed a young child of around two to three years exploring an unfamiliar environment but nearly always looking back to their parent for signs of encouragement or reassurance and may run back for a brief touch before going off to exploring again. This physical to and fro between the child and the parent is a further dimension to learning about being more independent while also learning about physical 'safe limits', which in turn leads into a growing understanding about *boundaries to behaviour*. The language we tend to use reflects our unconscious understanding of this process as we tell someone they need to 'know their limits' or someone has 'stepped over the mark', 'gone too far' and so on. However, once again, the way in which a child can respond to having limits imposed upon them and the way in which it is achieved will reflect on how the child will then face later challenges to their abilities to manage their own behaviour.

Bowlby's attachment theory emphasizes the child's fundamental need for feelings of security and safety which go beyond the physical (but which incorporate the sensory memories of such contact) and into the realm of the child's mental health and emotional well-being. He coined a term 'an internal working model' to describe the way in which we learn to view the world – in other words, our internal working model guides the way in which we feel about ourselves and how we approach or withdraw to new people and situations. He felt that this 'working model' (a term which implies a dynamic function) was built on the quality of the attachment relationship, and it was his colleague Mary Ainsworth who developed a system known as the 'strange situation' to assess the varying patterns of this relationship. Her three main patterns of attachment behaviour in the child (secure, insecure anxious and insecure avoidant) have been validated across a variety of cultures including potential links between anxious attachment and a range of developmental problems (Crittenden and Clausen, 2000). The effects of early attachment patterns have also been shown to influence relationships across the lifespan, with even some evidence to suggest continuation of attachment patterns across generations, such is the probable tenacity of these emotionally driven neural pathways.

Crittenden's view is that the basic principle around which much of our behaviour and our needs are organized is one of self-preservation and a guarding against danger. This is the other side of the same coin from thinking of our fundamental need for safety and security. However, the particular stance she takes is on how these patterns develop over time as the child gets older and how early patterns of security or insecurity and their various, perhaps more straightforward manifestations can become more complex and subtle or equally complex but more florid. Initially, of course, as she reminds us and which has been the basis of the previous information in this chapter, the child's distress is actually 'adaptive' as it ensures that care will arrive. It is the changing nature of the child as it grows older that brings with it an equal necessity for the parent also to adapt to these needs. The mother in the intense interaction of those early weeks provided an environment in which the requirements of the baby for emotional, physical, biological and physiological regulation predominated setting the early pathways of experience. As we shall see in Chapter 4, these changing requirements mean that different aspects of development become 'foreground' and others 'background' – but still maturing and developing, shifting and changing in the kaleidoscope that is developmental growth and maturation.

Chapter 4

Time-related emergence of skills and abilities, growth and change

This is the fourth of the overlapping frameworks for understanding behaviour. Trevarthen (2005, p.96) notes that:

> the evidence shows that age-related changes change parents' behaviour, teaching them to expect different behaviours from their infants, and to act differently in their support. Each relationship is a dynamic affair with its own history, but there are remarkable similarities, including differences between the timing of developmental changes for male and female infants, that cannot be explained as consequences of cultural ideas that shape parental responses.

Changes in behaviour linked to developmental shifts can occur at any age. For example, a teenager experiencing puberty will challenge previously accepted guidance and boundaries, investigate new experiences and struggle with conflicting needs for greater independence and reassurance/emotional safety. The teenager's behaviour will reflect physical, neurological/biochemical and psychological upheavals and it is the same for the child who is undergoing rapid shifts and changes in the early years. This chapter, therefore, considers these age related changes and how these also constitute a change in the way the child both experiences and understands the world.

These shifts in skills and abilities occur during widely acknowledged timeframes. Each phase builds on the one before it and so there is both change and continuity within any child's developmental trajectory. Such change brings with it new challenges and possibilities for both child and parent, especially the child's emerging independence. Each phase is also set in the context of the child's family, which may also be undergoing change, such as circumstances in the parents' own lives, the lives of siblings or the arrival of a new baby. The child's own widening experience of the world through attendance at playgroup, nursery or school and/or experiencing different types of alternative care also impact upon the child's ability to understand and manage their experiences.

To emphasize the elements of continuity as well as change, this chapter builds on the previous chapters with a brief revisit of those early weeks.

Tick tock – the relentless ticking of the developmental clock

Reference has been made previously to Bruce Perry's wry observation that we all may grow but not all 'grow up', and indeed this phrase is often heard – usually in times of great irritation – exhorting someone to 'grow up'. What we mean is that we want someone to behave differently, to behave more sensibly perhaps or more appropriately, but it may also reflect our expectations. Some of the issues that arise when thinking about behaviour are whether what we expect of children is actually appropriate for them, and it is here that understanding the developmental shifts and changes is so vital. Physical change and ageing is relentless: we cannot stop growing physically upwards to our genetically determined height and we cannot stop growing older whether we are six months or sixty years and experiencing all the particular bodily and hormonal changes associated with it. Nor can we stop the widening of experiences of both people and the environment, such as going to school, working, forming relationships. What is more open to change is our knowledge and understanding and our particular strategy for dealing with both the growing complexities of life in today's world and what surprises, both welcome and unwelcome, may be in store.

Whatever our life's trajectory, it is from the bedrock of the early weeks discussed in the previous chapter and summarized below that we move towards forming the picture we have of ourselves, our bodies and our environment, remembering always that the bedrock is formed (and continues to be so) on the particular levels experienced of love, acceptance and nurture.

The rest of this chapter has been organized to explore these developmental shifts and to consider the implications for adults of the child's changing needs and demands, how adult responses influence behavioural outcomes and how a child learns to manage their emotions. At the same time, we must remember that each developmental shift builds on previous experience, and so the quality of those experiences will have affected the particular maturational level reached. In addition, the child's own temperament and levels of cognitive ability will also play their part.

The skills and abilities identified in this chapter *broadly* reflect times of significant change, but it must be remembered that each child has their own developmental 'clock' so some children achieve expected changes earlier, while others may take longer. As Crittenden (2008) says, 'children mature continuously but unevenly.' However, there remains an expectation that typically developing children will mature in certain developmental areas along similar timelines as Trevarthen (2005) indicated above. Children with profound learning disabilities, of course, may take years to achieve even the most basic functions, but what must never be forgotten is that their emotional world is active, influencing behaviour in the same way as a child with more typical levels of cognitive ability. What they may require very long term is for adults to constantly help them to manage their emotions and to 'read' their behaviour as an integral part of their communication – just as adults must do for very young children.

Another aspect that will thread through the ensuing discussions is the acknowledgment of the reality of innate gender differences, as Trevarthen also indicated. It is possible that a lack of understanding of these differences can lead, for example, for some boys to be labelled as difficult and/or disruptive when they may be responding to inner distress because of inappropriate expectations.

A glance back

In Chapter 3, the relevance of the need for close companionship was discussed. In particular, the way in which nature appeared to set the scene for the beginnings of this relationship through the baby's familiarity with the mother's voice, coupled with reflex actions of rooting, grasping, sucking, startle and, of course, the baby's ability to express its needs through crying. The particular magic of the quality of the maternal voice when talking to babies was also discussed, together with its role in not only providing a soothing, attractive and joyful means of communication but also its influence on the baby's overall development through regulation of sensory stimulation and movement.

This also links back to the metaphor of thinking of life as a journey. This perspective may suggest that at different times in our life it is necessary for particular skills and abilities to be in place in order to achieve what is necessary for us to learn or achieve as human beings. For example, as we know, brain growth is the fastest within the first four years or so. Furthermore, within that period, it seems to be particularly dynamic within the first eighteen months to two years. But why is this, what is the significance of such rapid growth? What is the work/learning we have to do in order to be able to function well as a growing child and then an adult?

In the first instance, we have to adapt to life outside the womb and the particular focus in those early weeks, as discussed, appears to be on establishing the basic rhythms of life with feeding, sleeping, temperature control, movement coordination/organization, soothing of distress and establishing feelings of contentment. The rapidly growing brain is organizing the repetitive experiences into early patterns. This means that while the baby is experiencing their day-to-day care, they are also establishing who the important people are in their lives and building up a sensory and emotional map of what their world feels like to them. The individual pathways of fundamental levels of safety and security are being laid down. Therefore, it is certainly possible that those first three months of life outside the womb – sometimes called 'the fourth trimester' – is an *essential* period for close, intense contact between parents and baby, especially the mother as she is already 'primed' in her turn through, for example, hormonal influences and usually (as a female) greater sensitivity to facial expressions.

The suggested essential nature of this period may be because this is a time when babies learn the most fundamental lesson of all, which is that they are not alone. They learn this through being held but also because when they call, someone comes. Prolonged uncomforted crying can lead to the development of an 'over-sensitive stress response system' (Sunderland, 2006), and perhaps uncomforted crying is so stressful to the newly born baby because of the devastating nature of the earliest form of loneliness.

Such an 'over-sensitive stress response system' means that in later years a child who finds it difficult to cope with upset of any kind will react strongly in response to the horrible internal feelings. The *actual* behaviour will vary dependent on what the child has learned works for them, so some will become angry and disruptive while others may cling, whine, cry, while yet others may dampen down their feelings.

Another lesson in these very early weeks potentially contributes to the first emerging glimmers of being both a separate and a connected individual. This is the time when a baby is indiscriminate about who is caring for them, as they will be responsive to appropriate care by any adult. This is crucial for survival in case the mother is unwell or unable to care for any reason. However, the speculative early activity of mirror neurons allied to the capacity to imitate mouth movements by the baby, responsiveness to facial expressions, physical care and feeding as well as emotional nurturing will gradually lead to the greater discrimination of key people. Therefore, another essential lesson to learn appears to be 'who is it?' An interesting link is made by Chisholm (2007, p.174) when considering the indiscriminate friendliness of some Romanian adoptees. She notes that

> attachment by definition is a discriminating bond; such indiscriminate friendliness may be not unlike the indiscriminate behaviour displayed by infants prior to forming an attachment bond.

These children had been unable to form a relationship with any one particular person, and when adopted continued to find difficulty working out where their attachment security could lie. They unconsciously still seek a special person, but it becomes harder as they get older to tease away the influence of their experiences to go back to the heart of the matter. This need to find out 'who is who' possibly anticipates the first 'question' in play for finding out about objects, i.e. 'what is it?'. We need to be able to identify and discriminate between both people and things in order to provide a base for further understanding.[1]

For the typically developing child, as we saw in Chapter 3, a number of changes take place around the cusp of three months of age. For example, the capacity to imitate mouth movements appears to diminish, 'sticky fixation' is reduced and babies are enthusiastically reaching out both physically and metaphorically. So it seems the baby is now moving into the next phase of development, which is to widen both its social and environmental experiences while also 'firming up' knowledge of those key people.

A widening world – towards the child's first birthday

What is happening in the world of the baby who is now smiling, vocalizing, recognizing and preferring their key people to others but is still broadly friendly and accepting of strangers? What are they up to? What do they need? The important thing to recognize is that in these ensuing months the emotional well-being of the child is linked with *all* aspects of parental care. The 'internal working model' is being formed in response to this *association* between all the child's experiences, which is why, perhaps,

Crittenden (2008) prefers to think of this association of experiences as a 'potential neural network'. These are then attuned to heightened responses to particular experiences, which in turn reflect the responses to previous events.

This means that while the baby is now beginning to want to explore more, the need for emotional and physiological regulation by the parent doesn't go away. It is certainly true that as the child grows older, these needs usually become less intense and the child (and we) learn ways of coping, but we only have to think about situations in which we feel anxious, distressed, ill or fatigued and how such feelings can be soothed and comforted by the presence of someone loved or even the kindness of strangers, such as a nurse's brief handhold when a patient is about to go for an operation.

Lewis et al. (2000) describe our human physiology as both a closed and an open 'loop' system, i.e. we do have functions that do not rely on the presence of someone else. However, surprisingly perhaps, most of our human regulatory systems such as heart rate, hormone levels and even immune function are influenced by our interactions with others and especially so as infants when our experiences influence every part of the workings of our nervous system.[2] We need contact with others from cradle to grave; very few people can live in total isolation from others, and such deprivation has been used as the most severe (and feared) form of punishment for centuries. What all this means is that the growing baby, who has now hopefully established some of the basic rhythms of life in close and virtually constant contact with its mother, is ready for wider experiences but remains vulnerable. The growing child's needs for attuned care giving is just as vital but *different*.

For example, at around three to five months, babies with their greater ability to focus on things further away will become very excited at the sight of new objects and people. As Berry Brazelton (2006) charmingly puts it, babies are 'literally panting with anticipation when they see something new'.[3] He also reminds us that this new-found interest can also lead to sleeping disruption as the baby notices everything. He describes in particular how babies can become distracted by seeing something interesting while being fed, and the mother needs to be prepared to allow for this lessening of the intensity of their relationship. This can be quite painful for some mothers who have been used to the baby having absolute and preferred focus on her. Reddy (2008) has also noted this shift in attention in her studies as she notes that 'looking around the room . . . is absolutely a marker of infants in the lab at 3–4 months in contrast to infants gazing exclusively at the mother's face at 2 months' (p.116). She notes that in these circumstances it is the *parent* who engages in more stimulating interactions to bring back the focus of the baby who increasingly realizes the attention that is being paid to *them*.

For the parent, the bond with the child includes the strength to tolerate separations as the child grows older and more independent and so even in these very early weeks, the baby's newfound interests might provide a very early rehearsal for when the child is ready to move on to nursery or school and then later, ultimately, 'flies the nest' and leaves home ready to (almost) make a new life for themselves.

This is often the time when babies also want to reach for everything, refining through repetition their hand–eye coordination and adaptation of hand shape to what is being grasped and held. While it will still take some years (until around age four) before they can reach, grasp and manoeuvre a range of objects accurately, this is where it all begins and even has significance for the learning of self-regulation. This is because at around three to nine months babies appear to be making more conscious responses to their environment, such as their reactions to familiar people and reaching for a toy that attracts their attention. In other words, they are beginning to choose what to do, although this ability is still very much in its infancy.

How the mother feels about and is able to tolerate this subtle shift in the baby's attention and her responses to the baby's attempts at investigation will influence the quality of the relationship with the baby and the baby's attitudes to exploration. What people working with new mothers need to remember is the genuine pain at the sense of loss of such an intense relationship which may be felt and could cause a shift in the mother's moods and responses even if only temporarily.

Another big change that is on the horizon from about six months is yet another type of 'separation' for breastfeeding mothers. This is the time when the baby is moving on from being fully breastfed to starting on solids. Some mothers will welcome this stage while others again will feel a sense of loss that they are no longer the primary source of nutrition for their baby. In addition, the very distractability of the baby at this time can mean that some mothers may attempt to almost force their babies to eat when they want to play instead. This can result in mealtimes becoming mini battle grounds. How this process takes place and the emphasis placed on moving onto solids (or not) can set the scene for later attitudes to food and eating.

This is also a time when a baby's sleep can become disruptive, and links with later behaviour can be made when thinking about how a lack of sleep can lead to a child being disruptive or withdrawn. The ability to settle and feel comfortable when waking in the night has to be learned and supported. Babies sleep cycles are changing around this time and they can wake themselves through their own restlessness. Parents being supported in helping their babies through providing a soothing and consistent bed-time routine and quiet reassurance by low-key presence and gentle voice can help.

However, whatever the range of shifts in this period, including growing control of the trunk and finding the feet fascinating, teething and growing curiosity about the world, it is the parents' responses that guide the ongoing sense of self and perception of the environment. Parental reactions to this growing independence can vary greatly, with some parents not only welcoming but also wanting to *hurry* the child's developmental progress, which can be just as unhelpful for the baby as the parent who wants the baby to remain exclusively focused on her. Such reactions, as already mentioned in previous chapters, are part of the parents' own emotional world, and professionals who work with children and their families need to be sensitive to the variety of responses that may exist. They must always hold in mind, too, the knowledge that parental actions and reactions contribute constantly to the child's 'potential neural networks' that are being established. Parenting, therefore, increasingly includes not only responses to the child's emotional displays and nurture needs but also reactions to the quest for independence and to the child's curiosity and need to explore – which is running parallel to increasing physical and communicative ability.

The 'seeking' system described by Panksepp (1998)[4] is his suggestion that the 'mammalian brain' contains a system involved in a 'foraging/exploration/investigation/curiosity/interest/expectancy/SEEKING' system that leads organisms to eagerly pursue the fruits of their environment' (p.145).

This indicates the deep-seated nature of our wish to discover and to explore our environment, from tasting and mouthing objects as a baby to wanting to explore the universe as an adult. When one considers the child who is already 'turned off' learning and how this can close the door to all the worlds that could be open to him or her, we can see how the stifling of curiosity can have such long-term repercussions. Babies playing with their parents and also exploring by themselves are involved in 'focused attention', which linked with curiosity can help lay the foundations for later and different types of learning.

If we think about the focused attention of the newborn to its mother, and then later focused attention while exploring their environment or involved in games with their parents such as 'horsy horsy' or 'peek-a-boo', it allows concentration and an ability to attend to begin to take shape. In the same way that we need to experience loving care in order to develop our own capacity to give love, it is through opportunities to focus and *to be focused on* that the child is learning to 'pay attention'. This means that as older children and adults we are able to stay on task and/or retain interest while sitting in class, being in a cinema, listening to a lecture, doing our household bills and so on. The ability to stay reasonably focused while carrying out an activity is vital for all of us in all aspects of our lives, not just formal learning. The process seems to be that babies begin life by being very focused on their parent (because perhaps they need to be), and then become distracted by a newfound awareness of their surroundings. However, a parent's ability to follow their interest and at the same time help the baby to return to an activity such as feeding may have an influence on the child's ability to both inhibit a reaction and learn about shared interest.

Once again, we can see how parental and other adult responses to the child's need to explore and to engage their curiosity can support or dampen these processes at such an early stage. An infant who is left alone for long periods, spoken to briefly, put in front of a television for amusement or given very limited opportunity to watch the world go by, to feel and touch, is already having those innate systems rendered less and less active. The potential consequences will reverberate in the behaviour of the child in the nursery and in school – and in later life if no one tries to reignite the spark of curiosity and investigation. The potentially innate nature of curiosity and interest and its allied neurochemical activity in the brain may explain why those who are sad, disaffected or suffering from a sense of purposelessness can turn to cocaine or amphetamines. as these mimic this brain activity and allow feelings of interest and excitement to occur – in other words, they can feel *alive* again. Children and teenagers who partake in truly dangerous activities may also be trying to awaken this system, as might those who self-harm.

Many years ago, when working briefly in an alcohol rehabilitation unit as a counsellor, I remember a client whose arms were criss-crossed with healed cuts. When his reasons for harming himself were explored, he described how he only felt alive when he experienced the pain. What he seemed to be experiencing was not a sense of loss, which implies that something must have been experienced initially, but rather a sense of *absence* – a space where something should have been. It was through self-harm that he activated the release of opiods in his brain and thereby their action as both relieving pain and feeling soothed. Alcohol is also suggested to activate parts of the 'reward' systems in the brain and so his cocktail of self-harm and self-medication through alcohol temporarily gave him relief from his inner distress, most likely caused by his history of persistent neglect in childhood.

All in all, we must not underestimate the excitement of exploration for the child, with its resulting activation of such reward and emotional systems in the brain. This implies that not only finding out about people but also discovery of the workings of the environment is both rewarding and possibly necessary for emotional health.

As children move towards the latter part of the first year, a number of important shifts take place which seem to allow new perspectives to emerge. A particular example is a change in the way babies are able to remember, and the ability to find an object such as a toy which has been hidden in a *different place* begins to emerge. Children will also begin to look for a dropped object, and this is all part of the emergence of the concept of object permanence, which would tie in with a more complex memory system. A game such as 'peek-a-boo', which many parents almost instinctively appear to play with children around this age, is a wonderful, fun way of children learning that someone can 'disappear' behind a cloth and then 'reappear' as the same person. Children who are mobile around this age can also choose to go *towards* something, all the time coincidentally improving muscle control and hand–eye coordination, which also further supports the capability for independent choice.

This often means that the choice for the child is to follow their parent around everywhere, and this could be part of learning that mum in the kitchen is the same person when she is in the hall, the bedroom or the toilet. Some parents find this phase of being followed around irritating, while others sense that while this is partly to do with the baby wanting to be close to them, it is also part of something just as deep-seated, i.e. the realization that existence is permanent and continues even in absence. Such awareness needs practice in order to be established, and the ability to be mobile may be a timely coincidence to support such learning.[5]

The emergence of object permanence and its links with changes in the child's behaviour also tie in with the emergence of other important skills around this time, i.e. the ability to point and 'social referencing', and these also link together. The child learns to point in two ways: one is to point at something desired, such as a toy, and the other is to point to something with a burgeoning understanding that someone is going to share the excitement with you. These types of pointing are known as *imperative* and *declarative* respectively.

The baby's realization that an object of interest can be shared is a truly wonderful shift in ability, and is built on all the interactions that have gone before, especially the awakening of different foci of attention at around three to four months. This 'sharing' and linking of minds, which is now not just between the child and parent but in a triangle of adult/child/interest, adds to both the widening of the world in which we can connect and awareness of being an individual, i.e. 'I can look, you can look, *we* can look' – what joy! Social referencing in its turn builds on this process as the child turns to the parent to gauge their reaction to someone or something unfamiliar. The child then adapts their behaviour according to the response of the parent. For example, if the mother shows a warm welcome to an unfamiliar person, the child will relax and be prepared to be friendly.

This is particularly noticeable in this latter half of the first year because this is also when 'stranger anxiety' emerges, and so the parent's understanding of this new-found awareness of familiar and unfamiliar will help the child cope with their anxious feelings.

Prior and Glaser (2007) note that the most probable period for developing stranger wariness is in the first three years of life, with it first occurring in typically develop-ing children at around eight months of age. They also posit that if children do not form selective attachments by around three years, 'children may become disinhibited in their approach to strangers', which reflects the findings of Chisholm's (2007) study discussed early in this chapter.

The emergence of 'stranger anxiety' pulls together the ongoing formation and quality of attachment security, the infant's ability for facial processing[6] and the 'use' of the adult to establish the safety or not of the particular context. In other words, not only is the baby discriminating between familiar, trusted and safe situations and the unknown, but the baby is also using the adult to establish if there is *danger* inherent in this new situation. A recent study by McElwain (2006), based on mother/infant interaction findings from the National Institute of Child Health and Human Development (NICHD) in the United States, strongly suggested that it was attentiveness to *distress* which seemed to be a prime factor in the formation of secure attachments to the mother rather than level of sensitivity of response in other situations such as play, feeding and so on. While this study was considering the formation of attachments overall, nevertheless the implication may be that responses to the child's wariness or actual distress at the appearance of strangers during this phase may also provide a further substrate for more fine-tuning of the quality of the attachment formation.

Of course, the child's own temperament will come into play as some children are more naturally outgoing and less troubled by events while others are more shy or with-drawn. However, in both circumstances with appropriate, responsive care a child can still overcome their fears whether transitory or more intense. As this is also the phase when the child's attachment patterns become well-established towards their significant adults, so separations from the mother especially can cause great distress and this can continue for many months.

Occurring in parallel with these changes is a surge of connections between the limbic system and a particular part of the frontal cortex known as the 'orbitofrontal region' in the latter half of the first year. If we remember that it is the right hemisphere of the brain which is more dominant during the first two years or so of life, so it is the right orbitofrontal region which appears to be most involved in self-regulation which helps inhibit reactions. For example, when faced with an unfamiliar person, the child's amygdala will respond and send signals of possible threat to all the allied bodily networks which become activated in such situations, i.e. raised heart rate, blood pressure and chemical and hormonal changes.

The orbitofrontal cortex is the area where such signals can be modified, and so when baby turns to mother or hides their face and mum comforts and behaves in a welcoming manner, this helps the pathways between amygdala and orbital frontal cortex to be developed, thereby calming and reassuring the baby (Schore, 2003). Incidentally, Schore also notes that 'the same system that is shaped by the attachment relationship regulates aggression' (p.122).

If we pull all this together, we can see that the parental responsiveness to the needs of the baby is going to contribute to the shaping of these neural networks, which are exquisitely adaptable to the particular psychological and physical environment in which the child is growing. Of course such adaptiveness also means that if parental care is neglectful, careless, intermittent or abusive in other ways the child can respond to positive interventions, and so these pathways while crucial can be modified – although the later such interventions occur, the more difficult the process.

All this suggests to me that if a baby in the first year of life is not protected, care for, responded to and cuddled, does not get talked to very often and is simply left more or less to its own devices or the unresponsive attention of a television, then the ultimate lack of basic regulation of mind, heart and body will lead to a terrible, wordless loneliness. This is a loneliness which is a space in the psyche where the growing sense of a loveable self should be.

This 'gap' in the emotional world of the child will lead to the adaptation of behaviours which work towards gaining the acceptance so much desired, such as compulsive caregiving and/or wanting to please others, with very little confidence in challenging and/or complaining. For such children – and adults – rejection in any form is often very difficult to deal with and they respond accordingly. For others, their strategy could be a denial of their need for other people, withdrawing emotionally from others appearing cold and perhaps uncaring of the feelings of others. However, such needs will out and some will turn to others who are similar in their strategies and needs, or be attracted to those who provide a distorted mirror image of what they want so much and missed. An example would be membership of a gang with its tight rules, strong hierarchy and sense of belonging to those on the 'inside'. Drugs and/or alcohol are another route for some, while yet others may try to fulfil these needs through academic and/or financial success. Some people in adult life may feel they just 'tick along' with vague feelings of 'is this all there is' pervading their lives. Ultimately, it is all on a spectrum and the degree to which children and adults adopt a particular strategy will be influenced by life's opportunities in education, jobs and support.

Crittenden's (2007) dynamic model of maturation (DMM)[7] describes such adaptations over time. In this she puts forward her hypothesis as to how attachment classifications of secure and insecure (with its subdivisions of anxious and avoidant) are fluid, and that individuals do not always fit neatly into a particular pattern. For example, she notes that experience leads to both 'change and continuity in the patterns of attachment' with three kinds of change possible:

1   change from one pattern to another (i.e. from secure to insecure and vice versa)
2   change in the array of possible strategies
3   change from simple substrategies to more complex and sophisticated substrategies within a dominant pattern. (p.343)

Her starting point is that while attachment patterns can be strongly identified at around twelve to fourteen months, the levels of an infant's abilities do not correlate with those of the older child and adult, and therefore they cannot use the types of behaviours that are available to us all as we get older. For example, we may feel very hurt, but we have learned to hide it and protect ourselves from further hurt in one way or another. Even a school-age child can either hide his or her feelings or exaggerate them, or they can do, think and say different things. Crittenden's example of the latter is that a child can appear to be happily playing while in reality, working out how to 'snitch forbidden cookies from the kitchen'. In other words, our capacity to deceive grows. Such a realization that a child's fundamental feelings of security and confidence or insecurity can have a range of behaviours which may accompany a basic sense of emotional loneliness is very important for adults who work with children, and can sound a warning note to those who try to classify a child's behaviour in absolute terms of their potential secure or insecure attachment.

In addition, as Crittenden points out, as infants we have no control over the people we meet or the contexts in which we find ourselves. As toddlers and preschoolers become increasingly more mobile and strive for independence, as discussed in the next section, they can begin to be able to choose friends (or whom they want to have as a friend), and there is increasingly more choice in where they can go within different contexts. At nursery or preschool, a wider and wider range of people are encountered, Crittenden notes that at school the influences of a child are 'increasingly beyond the range of parents'. Children also increasingly *encounter the behaviour of others*, which provides them with insight into not only how other children may behave but also other adults – whom children continue to monitor closely.

Finally in this section, a word about memory because the realization that something not seen can still exist also indicates a growing complexity in the child's memory system, which links with the increasing realization of loss when a loved adult leaves for whatever reason. As infants we certainly do remember, but our memories consist mainly of the patterns of emotional and sensory experience. However, Meltzoff (2002b) has shown that babies can use 'imitative games to check the identity of the person in front of them', but this capacity to remember something from time past and to 'hold the knowledge' for sufficient time to act on that knowledge is part of what is termed 'working memory'. This may also represent the first (unconscious) awareness of something that is both past and present.

Essentially, there appear to be two types of memory: long-term and working memory just mentioned. Long-term memory is itself divided into explicit or declarative memory and implicit or unconscious memory, which also includes procedural memory. Procedural memory, which is present in infants according to Crittenden et al. (2007), 'encodes information as sensorimotor schemata' and therefore includes patterns of 'familiar, preconscious patterns of behaviour'. Procedural memory is also involved in how we learn to do things such as walking, dancing, driving a car, knitting or adapting our grasp to various sized objects,[8] Emotions also influence what is remembered from the amount of sensory information received and the related feeling responses help attract, maintain or lose attention. The shift in being able to remember the unseen implies a possible surge in working memory capacity so that the awareness of a continuous thread of life becomes more apparent. People and things do not simply appear and disappear but are part and parcel of existence – we need to be able to remember what has just been and what is occurring at the moment and therefore what we can act upon. The baby searching for the hidden toy is learning a momentous truth about life which is that it exists in a range of physical and abstract dimensions – space and time.

Our more conscious or explicit memory becomes active only when we achieve verbal skills as this relies on language. This type of long-term memory includes what we know (or think we know), our beliefs (semantic memory), together with our memory for events, termed 'episodic memory'. Crittenden et al. suggest that this type of memory emerges later than semantic memory as most people are unable to recall events before the age of three, though of course there are always exceptions.

Entering the second year and towards preschool

The second year of life, from about fourteen months onwards, for many children marks a significant sea change in the child's abilities. However, we have to remember that children remain vulnerable to stress, so that a new baby in the family, a house move, changes within the family, can all lead to a child regressing in their behaviour in one way or another. Children appear to lose their newfound skills, returning to ways in which they perhaps feel more safe and secure. The other point to remember is that children's development is uneven both within an individual child and between children, so within the onward march of development there are also some 'bumps' and possible side alleys.

Perhaps the greatest indication of this sea change is of growing independence, which is allied to the growing understanding of a physical, active self within a body over which the child has greater control. This sense of independence has begun with the ability to choose a toy and to choose the person to be with (or at least make feelings known). The ability to sit independently towards the latter part of the first year allowed the free use of the hands, which meant greater opportunities for exploration and play. In the second year, this is supported by increasing mobility, with most children walking independently. The ability to walk is one of the great markers of development that underpins the child's capacity to have greater freedom of movement and to begin to voluntarily explore the environment – under the watchful gaze of adults. The emergence of babbling at around eight months now moves into the child being able to say a few recognizable words, and it is evident that comprehension is greater than word count.

Berry Brazelton and Sparrow (2006) point out a very interesting facet of this growing independence which is that, even at twelve months, the child is showing wariness of contact with strangers. This is thought to be not just because of stranger anxiety but also because, as the child is more aware of a body that is theirs, there is an instinctive and growing need to place a boundary on interactions. Children's displays of wariness therefore can serve a purpose, which is to send a signal to adults to give the child time to gain confidence. They have a growing awareness of their body and how they move within the space that surrounds them, what they approach and what they avoid – all the time observing and monitoring the actions of others.

As a paediatrician, Berry Brazelton has to examine many one-year-olds and just above, and he has noticed that eye contact can appear threatening to many children of this age., As a 'stranger' and furthermore someone who is possibly about to do something to the child, he sees the need is to approach cautiously and to be respectful of the child's 'fear of being invaded'. For many children entering this second year of life, new experiences are something that can provoke a great deal of wariness before the child settles comfortably, which is something that perhaps adults do not always take into consideration, especially when introducing a very young child to a new situation. Boundaries are a very interesting concept, and perhaps we need to establish physical boundaries, i.e. about our bodies and what we can and cannot do, before we are ready to understand the more abstract concepts of boundaries to our actions. For example, it may be that it is not until we are able to physically stop, such as when running – which is very difficult and needs help from adults – that we are also able to understand what 'stop' means when this instruction refers to different aspects of our behaviour.

Berry Brazelton also notes that 'the coming months are full of passionate striving to do everything (she) can on her own' and this wariness and/or protest at doing something or going somewhere the child doesn't want, at that moment, is part of this picture of gaining independence and control. However, just as in the teenager described at the beginning of this chapter, the need for *dependence* as well as independence is equally strong and it is this conflicting need which produces what are usually termed 'tantrums', a key feature of children approaching two years of age.

Before we turn to tantrums, a brief summary of all the changes that occur in the second year of life highlight just what an intense, fascinating and sometimes fearful time it must be for the child. As mentioned above, words are emerging and combined with gestures the child is more able to make their own needs known and be more aware of what others want too. Mobility is increasing apace with the widening experience of their surroundings that comes with it. Other things are happening too, such as the awareness that others may have likes and dislikes different from their own. For example, Gopnik et al. (1999) describe their famous 'broccoli experiment' with children aged around fourteen months and others around eighteen months.[9] Children were presented with two bowls, one filled with tasty crackers and the other with raw broccoli. The researcher then expressed her delight in raw broccoli and disgust at the crackers. When the children were asked to give her some of her favourite food, the younger children still gave her crackers while the older children, reliably around eighteen months, handed her the broccoli. These eighteen-month-olds had realized that someone else may dislike what they love and vice versa.

The timing of this knowledge is interesting because it is at around fourteen months that many children begin to recognize themselves in a mirror, point to their own body parts and identify themselves as a boy or a girl (although they often don't realize that they are always going to be a boy or a girl until around four years). This bodily awareness is supported by a more conscious awareness of what the body is actually doing, and so begin to be aware of those signals that mean they need to pass urine or open their bowels. This is accompanied by a general fascination with all their bodily parts, and children will want to feel and explore what they can see when undressed. It is as if they need to get to know their bodies, and again parental attitudes to this exploration will be influential in forming attitudes to the body and its functions.

It is also certainly possible that being aware of those sensations as coming from both outside and *inside the self* may also help to learn that feelings which indicate an emotion also come from *within* the self and can be understood as being part of the self.

Towards the end of this second year, it also becomes more obvious that children are able to understand that someone can have a feeling that *they don't have* at that particular moment *but* that they can recognize it *and* react to it. For example, they can see someone upset and offer their teddy to provide comfort. Gopnik et al. (1999) also provide a very succinct definition of empathy: 'not just knowing that other people feel the same way you do; it's about knowing that they don't feel the same way and caring anyway' (p.39). Children towards the end of their second year appear to be able to grasp this concept regarding feelings, although they still are not able to take the *physical perspective* of someone else for another year, i.e. a two-year-old can 'hide' behind a curtain but not realize that they can still be seen if only their face is concealed.[10] The charming way that children of this age will also close their eyes and believe you can't see them because they can't see you is another example. However, by around three years, children have learned that there are differences between what they can see and what someone else can, and it is also around this time that there is a growing emphasis in children's play around fantasy and role play. It is fascinating that bodily and emotional awareness seems to precede beginning to get into the *mind* of someone else, which in turn is supported by the different perspectives that can be adopted in their play.

The capacity for pretend has emerged around fourteen months and for some children earlier as they begin to talk on a toy telephone, drink from tiny cups or bath teddy. This type of pretend seems to be an extension of imitation as the children use props to act out daily life experiences, and imitation is also used as a powerful means of communication between children. The emergence of pretend also seems to run parallel to a surge in the levels of imitation by children of adult actions. Children of this age will even imitate styles of walking of their parents. While patterns of walking are laid down uniquely for each individual, family members will notice that there are also styles within a family which can be recognizable in certain ways of moving. In addition, boys will tend to imitate how their fathers walk and girls their mother's. This linking with the same gender parent is probably part of the awareness of who they are and also very broadly corresponds with the timing of mirror recognition. Therefore this surge in the child imitating the adult is also helping to establish an important part of their identity.

Gradually over time this type of play develops in complexity and sophistication as children increasingly adapt props to represent something else. For example, instead of talking into a toy telephone, they will use a banana or later still a twig or a brick, and later still perhaps nothing at all, simply the hand to the ear. Such play presupposes a knowledge and understanding of the realities of the properties of objects and their continuing existence – in other words, in order to use objects as props or representations for something else, a child has to be grounded in an understanding of the real world (including the permanence and continuity of the properties of objects).

Joy, tears, temper tantrums and 'little Neros'

All these changes in the second year mean challenges for both children and their parents and other carers. Not only are there changes in the way the child understands the world and the people in it, but there are also greater physical and verbal capabilities with increasing comprehension and the ability to follow *simple* instructions. However, as well as this increasing compliance, there is another side to the coin. The wariness of the younger child has already been mentioned, as has the passionate striving to try to do everything oneself – no wonder there are frustrations as well as episodes of great and exuberant joy! Margot Sunderland, in her excellent book *The Science of Parenting* provides a particularly compassionate, as well as realistic, view on temper tantrums, which she describes as 'storms of feeling'. This description is probably much more accurate than 'tantrum', with all its negative connotations of being inherently bad and requiring control. Sunderland also reminds us that these storms are not only frightening for the child but also for adults, especially if those adults find it difficult to cope with their own intense feelings. As young children have a particular tendency to have a storm in a public place, parents also have to cope with feeling under scrutiny by others, and again their own levels of confidence will influence how they react.

However, it is not just parents, of course, who can have varied responses to the screaming, distressed child but also those working with children on a regular basis, and as free places for two-year-olds are coming into force in Britain, there are increasing numbers of these children entering day care just when they are going through the wealth of profound changes alluded to in this chapter. There are always challenges for practitioners at whatever age a child will come into their care, but two-year-olds bring with them the reputation of the 'terrible twos' and so there may already be an expectation in the minds of professionals that this is something they are going to have to deal with.

What might help parents and practitioners is the knowledge and understanding that the expression of these tantrums or storms is that they are an essential part of growing up. In addition, Sunderland points out that there are two types of tantrum, one of which arises out of genuine overwhelming distress and frustration, the 'temper tantrum', and the second she terms the 'little Nero' tantrum. The first is the one that requires comforting and solace, while the second is an indication for the adult to be in charge.

Temper tantrums – those storms

If you recall, there is a surge in brain connections between the limbic centres in the brain to the orbitofrontal cortex (the bit just above your eyes) at around eight months, but this surge continues into the latter part of the second year. These connections are to do with inhibiting the activation of distress networks of rage, pain and fear (Schore, 1994; Panksepp, 1998; Karr-Morse and Wiley, 1997; Sunderland, 2006), and these networks need to be consolidated and strengthened. With many two-year-olds, we have children who also need regulation of these genuinely strong and powerful emotions through the understanding of the adults around them. This is not to say that adults cannot feel cross, frustrated and fed up themselves, but again it is the adult's responsibility to see the reason for the behaviour. Such an approach often helps to deal with the situation more constructively than simply seeing the child as bad or naughty, or even terrible.

This phase is a truly important one in becoming a caring and empathic human being who is able to manage their emotions and have awareness of those of others. The child needs to find out that strong emotions can be both tolerated and resolved by the adult being able to understand the frustration and disappointment of not being able to have this toy or that biscuit. On the other hand, trying to *reason* with a child in such distress is simply useless. No matter how trivial the reason may seem to the adult, the distress means that even the most verbally advanced child will have great difficulty saying how they feel. Furthermore, they will certainly not be able to take in what is being said. If we recall how difficult it is to explain why we are crying – even as adults – perhaps we can identify with how the child feels when confronted by an adult demanding logic. Trying to stay calm and soothing the child with simple, comforting words will be more helpful. Some children will like being held, others not, especially if they are in a rage as well as distressed. If the situation has not escalated into full-blown distress, then distraction can work as can minimizing the situations, such as presenting clear choices when the child is getting dressed for example.

Little Neros

'Little Nero' tantrums is the term Sunderland has used to describe those behaviours which really are intended to 'control and manipulate' the parents and other adults. With the distress temper tantrum the child is at the mercy of his or her emotions and needs help to establish essential regulatory pathways in the brain. With the little Neros (who are both boys *and* girls) the behaviour is much more intentional in that, it is done to achieve a brief sense of control and perhaps a degree of predictability in the response of the parents. It can also be suggested that there is an element of seeking some sort of consistency in cause and effect, i.e. I scream and I get what I want.

The difference between these two states is quite marked as the child's anger is usually without tears and the ability to communicate is not lessened. It is this type of tantrum that is the one that adults are advised to ignore (so long as the child is safe). However, again reasoning is not an option as the adult can get drawn into an argument, which is in itself rewarding for the child. I wonder how many people recognize the situation, not just with children, when arguments simply go round and round with nothing achieved but with attention entirely focused on the child (or adult) who is not complying.

Generally in this type of situation any attention achieved either through anger, reasoning or explanations feeds the bullying tactic as the child realizes that they can get attention (as well as the currently desired item) through their commands and demands. The problem is that if such behaviour is allowed to succeed, then the toddler becomes the child who demands and tries to command other children and then the teenager who learns that the more they escalate their behaviour, the more others will give in, and as an adult, that bullying and hectoring are a way of getting what one wants – although, of course, it is never truly satisfying except briefly.

The reason that tantrums or storms of whatever kind are so common in the second to third year of life is because of the myriad changes that are occurring and the need for the child to understand and regulate the particularly strong and powerful feelings that are occurring as they experience boredom, frustration and disappointment. These feelings are linked to the feelings of growing power and independence, and children need to learn about boundaries so that eventually they can learn to self regulate. It is sometimes very hard for parents and other adults to recognize the responsibilities they have in helping the very young child to traverse the new emotional landscape with all the challenges that arise when encountering an increasingly wider range of experiences. However, children need to feel confident that adults can contain and manage the child's emotions and are not overwhelmed by them.

Sometimes, of course, adults *are* overwhelmed by the demands of their child or children, and so help from friends and family and of course professionals in early years can be a source of great comfort and relief. This can be especially helpful when they realize that a temper tantrum is a normal and necessary part of growing up. They then may be able to feel more confident about responding to these needs even when the child is also trying to get their own way by testing boundaries with their demands. They can also think about what situations seem to particularly trigger tantrums of either type. A child who is tired and/or hungry or is living in a household where the adults are already stressed will often be more prone to such outbursts of emotion, as of course will be a child who has not received comfort and attention in their infancy. However, it is obviously not always possible to pre-empt situations which may elicit the child's distress and frustration because what will upset the two-year-old can often be unpredictable or, as said earlier, seem incredibly trivial to adults. However, we need to remember that a two-year-old is a two-year-old and their view on life reflects their developmental level.

The other facet is the child's own temperament as some children will be much more placid while others much more irritable and therefore easily frustrated. For these children, there is a degree of risk that they may be more easily labelled naughty or difficult. Other children who might also receive this label are children who appear rather fearless or bold, and their constant striving to explore may also mean parents are constantly watchful and wary of danger. For some parents, they will delight in the adventurous nature of their child, but others may simply see the behaviour as challenging to them. This can engender a vicious circle of the child's frustrations being met with anger and/or hostility, which will then increase those panic/fear/rage systems that Panksepp (1998) has surmised exist in the human brain. In such situations, the unmet need for adult understanding and containment of these powerful fluctuations in mood can lead to chronic anger and possible aggression.

This period reminds me of the intensity of the first three months of life when a baby's first distress calls are responded to and the type and quality of the response helps the regulation of their very immature emotional and physiological systems. As Karr-Morse and Wiley (1997) describe, once soothed, the 'chemistry of alarm' in the baby's brain is 'brought back into balance'. The soothing response creates that map of neural responses – the neural footprint – which brings reassurance and later helps build the capacity to calm, self-soothe and ultimately a greater ability to cope. Just as the newborn needs to experience both a cessation of and a resolution to their needs, so that in a very profound way they learn that these feelings are not endless, so the child in the throes of the temper tantrum can learn that these feelings will cease and positive feelings can re-emerge.

However, while tantrums are a common and most probably an essential part of this phase of life, the frequency and level of distress displayed will vary from child to child. Some children, as indicated earlier, are more placid and therefore may be able to tolerate frustrations more easily. However, there may be some children whose displays of any kind of defiance or frustration are very low-key or rare, and for some this may be because they have already learned to dampen down their emotions because of the level of hostility of adult reactions. Rather than becoming more distressed and angry, these children tend to internalise these strong emotions – they still have them but they are turned inwards rather than outwards. Such children can seem very easy children to be with, but their compliance comes at a psychological cost, with poor self-esteem and a lack of confidence and/or fearfulness. Children who are born with a rather timid and fearful temperament may be the children who are most likely to adopt this pattern if their initial displays of emotion are met with irritation or ignored or castigated.

Ultimately, this phase of emotional storms seems to be the next essential stage in learning how to deal with the feelings brought about by a wider range of experiences and sets the stage for how the child will be able to face later challenges. There is so much they need to learn and are learning during this period, which is in many ways a dress rehearsal for the emotional disarray of puberty. Adult reactions to the child's displays of genuine feeling and accompanying levels of stress will either help or hinder them in dealing with their emotions influencing their reactions to frustration and stress as they get older. Therefore, adult responses will start to shape the kinds of behaviours that become foreground and background in the child's temperament, and especially so at these particular times in the child's development. The ability of adults to adapt to the child's style of behaviour is so important. For example, the innately timid child can still be 'stretched beyond their self-imposed limitations' (Karr-Morse and Wiley, 1997) if given enough time and support to have confidence in new situations, even if they may retain a frisson of anxiety at such times. On the other hand, the bold, fearless child can be encouraged to find ways of expressing this characteristic in ways that are positive, such as in very active, physical activities. Such children also need strong, fair, firm and consistent boundaries so that their boldness is not confounded by impulsivity and/or aggression.

In other words, the child's basic temperament is influenced by their experiences for good or ill. Because children and their emotional and social contexts are individual to them, their responses to their experiences will manifest along a spectrum of both levels of aggression and/or fearlessness or timidity/fearfulness and the kinds of situations which will trigger the behaviour. However, those children acting towards the more worrying ends of either end of the spectrum, without caring intervention will embed these patterns and as they get even older will become more difficult to alter.

Moving out of the storm

When children get older the storms subside somewhat in frequency and intensity, usually as the child approaches their third birthday. However, they will still find it hard to control their behaviour, for example the bed in the bed shop will look very inviting for a spell of jumping. The caring adult will be mortified, but children need help in realizing where it is alright to bounce on beds or that trampolines and playgrounds are more acceptable. Children have a very hard time working out which parts of their behaviour are acceptable or not in which context. Running, for example, is fine outside but not perhaps indoors. The key to all this is what has been indicated earlier: adults have to recognize that the child has an immature brain with regulatory pathways which still need to be supported in order to be established. This process does not happen by default. Sometimes it is hard for adults to realize just how long this whole process takes, and it is often not until the child is over five that they are able to really think about what options they might have.

However, the foundations for such skills are laid in these preschool years and the opportunities for children's independence, learning about boundaries and understanding the minds as well as the hearts of others lie not only in their day-to-day relationships with adults and peers but also in their opportunities for play as mentioned above. The particular element of play which comes into its own at around three years of age is the growing importance of fantasy and role play.

Flights of fancy

As we already know, play is common to all mammals and some birds, and children engage in playful exchanges as well as playing/exploring on their own, and later in parallel and then in cooperation with others. The capacity to play or be playful on one's own is a thread that remains throughout the developmental trajectory of play, from the earliest type of exploratory play to the more complex and abstract, which is fantasy and role play. Here again, the child's temperament may influence play preferences not only in type but also in degree of companionship. Some children may always prefer to play with perhaps one or two others and never really enjoy large group or team games.

Awareness of such differences in preference is important as sometimes there may be an expectation that *all* children will enjoy certain types of play or always be content to play with others. Awareness of gender-influenced tendencies towards different play themes is also important.

The mention of play themes brings us back to the emergence of fantasy and role play and the timing of this phase provides interesting speculation as to its essential nature. As far as is known, only humans engage in fantasy play and together with the ability to pretend itself, indicates a child's ability to use symbolic representation, i.e. that one thing can stand for another. This understanding is essential for the ability to read and write in tandem with physical, visual and hand–eye readiness.

The ability to adopt a fantasy role and play such games with others requires that in addition to understanding the properties of objects, there is also the capacity to communicate, to understand the likes and dislikes of others, to understand at some level the feelings of others. In order to play cooperatively, children also need to appreciate the goal-directed actions of others as well as what the child wants to achieve themselves, and children have usually reached this understanding by the early months of the second year (Meltzoff, 2002a; Gattis et al., 2002). Thinking back to the changes in that second year, we can see how skills are in place for the surge in cognitive as well as emotional understanding through the medium of fantasy play. In such play, children imitate the common phrases, behaviour and attitudes of the adults in their family. From this, they can then move on to add their own twist to the situations as their play becomes more self-determined and wider in context, embracing more characters, for example from television or films and thereby also more situations.

Children of around three to four years have a natural preoccupation with themselves and so fantasy and role play allows them to 'de-centre' and begin to try out what it might mean to be someone else. This is something that is crucial for the further development of empathy and the understanding that other people might have thoughts and ideas that are different from their own – a concept that can be reliably tested at around four to four and a half years.[11] Lillard (2002) provides a comprehensive overview of the links between pretend play and cognitive development but also notes that research indicates that securely attached children are more likely to engage in pretend play early and that 'secure attachment is also associated with better theory of mind performance'. 'Theory of mind' is the hypothesis presented by Alan Leslie (1987) regarding the ability to understand the thoughts/perspectives of another. It can be seen that fantasy/role play pulls together both emotional and cognitive aspects of the child's development, but here again the child's emotional world influences their capacity to play. For example, Panksepp (1998), while emphasizing that play is a 'primary emotional function of the mammalian brain' also found that negative emotions such as fear, as well as hunger, in animals 'can temporarily eliminate play'. For example, young chimpanzees 'after several days of isolation . . . become despondent and are likely to exhibit relatively little play when reunited' (p.282) Comparisons can be found with the diminished capacity for play in human children when upset and/or fearful, and this seems to apply to all types of play. My own small study of play in troubled children demonstrated this very clearly. The lack of general playfulness and in particular the absence of pretence of this kind was striking. Such findings suggest that there is a necessity for a child to feel emotionally secure in order to play imaginatively.

The absence of such play in a child should sound warning bells for adults as there will be a reason behind it, whether because of delayed cognitive ability or because of some emotional upset in one way or another. The importance of fantasy play with its rich associations with language, role taking, negotiation and emotional exploration as well as cognitive learning needs to be emphasized, and a child who does not play in this fashion is also probably communicating a need of some kind. There is something in the child's world which will not allow them to leave reality behind – no matter how briefly – and step into a world of fantasy.

However, it is important to remember that adults need to be aware of not just fantasy play but the level, quality, type and persistence of the content of the child's play in any of its forms as this can provide a window into the emotional world of the child and their levels of understanding.

I'm so afraid – the emergence of fears and phobias, and aggression

As we have seen, as the child grows older, not only skills and abilities change but also contexts and, most probably, encounters with a wider range of people and their families, including pets. Children very likely become aware of how small they are, and I wonder if this understanding of size comparison is supported by the urge which happens around now to 'dress up', especially in adult clothing. Hence the little girl tottering around in mum's shoes or the boy wearing dad's jacket. This widening of horizons also brings with it an awareness that there are potential dangers, and many children can develop fears and phobias about loud noises, dogs, going to specific places such as the doctor's surgery or the dark. Three-year-olds also develop aggressive feelings (both girls and boys), and these are different from the tantrum but are part and parcel of a widening range of more complex emotions, such as the jealousy of a new sibling. Such jealousy and rivalry can re-emerge at different stages of the *sibling's* development as the parents will have to adapt to those changing needs too. Children can also begin to suffer nightmares around this time and it may be that these new, strong feelings are being 'worked out' in dream time as well as during the day. Just as the child needs support and help during their temper tantrums, so does the child need help and understanding as new, strong feelings begin to emerge. Understanding that aggressive feelings emerge at around three years of age does not mean tolerating or accepting aggression, but it does indicate another challenge for the adult who, while recognizing its natural occurrence, needs to help channel such feelings positively. Adult role modelling of dealing with anger and aggressive feelings in a safe way and that such feelings can be controlled is crucially important for the child. Research such as the Dunedin longtitudinal study in New Zealand, which was of 1,000 children, found that children defined as at-risk at three years of age were twice as likely to be involved in 'criminally violent and abusive behaviour' (Zeedyk, 2009).[12] It is frightening to think that at such an early age, poor outcomes may be already on the horizon without positive interventions.

The very importance of peer relationships from about the second year onwards means that there will also be rivalries and tensions as children begin to negotiate being with a range of other children – which again is supported by playing fantasy or role play with a common theme such as pirates or going to the shops. The skills of being able to share and take turns are all difficult for such young children and yet adult expectations of these abilities are often high, causing tension and disappointment leaving children feeling frustrated when they simply don't really understand what is required. Outbursts of aggression or a reversal to temper tantrums continues during this third year as the child struggles to learn the limits to their behaviour and so the learning of the important lesson of how to control strong emotions. Adult understanding and consistency plus fairness of response and boundaries all help the child extract the 'rules of engagement', and that is what the child's brain is doing too. It is through repeated experiences that those neural pathways begin to be established, but it is the frequency and consistency of different aspects of the experience which provide the knots in the neural net of circuits and pathways, shaping the outcome, which is the child's day-to-day behaviour.

Summary

We want children to learn to be kind to one another, to share, to comply with instructions, but we want to ensure that we do not suffocate the child's feelings of curiosity and sense of independence either. Understanding the changing needs of children as they get older is all part of this balancing act of providing boundaries and freedom, safety and a degree of risk, nurturing and yet allowing the child to move on to make new friends and be comfortable with other people. We also need to be aware of what the child can actually manage, and also of any gender differences that may influence the way in which a particular child may experience the world. We need to have awareness of our own behaviour, remembering how closely children both imitate and monitor what we do and say. So it is now time to think in more detail about the role of the adult, and this is the focus of Chapter 5.

Chapter 5

The adult

Awareness, sensitivity, interpretation and responses

This chapter pulls together information from the preceding chapters and shifts the focus towards adult roles and responsibilities in various contexts, including grief and loss. Although reference has been made to the role of parents as appropriate throughout, in this chapter the scope is widened to consider in more detail the role of professional practitioners working with children and their families.

What is important for both parents and professionals is how adults interpret the child's behaviour and, so far, we have looked at a series of suggested frameworks which can support understanding. However, interpretation is also influenced by the adult's own emotional world, and for practitioners there is an additional dimension, i.e. the particular professional lens through which they observe the child. Gender also has a crucial role to play, and adult awareness of this issue is essential regarding their expectations of boys and girls and their understanding of how gender may influence patterns of behaviour as has already been alluded to in Chapters 3 and 4.

Furthermore, adults must try to remember that the child is constantly interpreting adult actions and intentions according to their levels of understanding – which are not necessarily linked to either chronological age or cognitive ability. Instead, the child's emotional experiences will play a powerful part in how well they can actually grow up.

This chapter will reflect on these issues and concludes with a discussion of broad principles regarding creating a positive environment for children and families, whatever the particular setting.

It may be true (and personally I think it is) that the quality of the first attachment relationships remains at the core of the human psyche across the lifespan. However, as we have seen in Chapter 4, the particular patterns of behaviour that reflect this quality are not static but can adapt and change according to circumstance, age and levels of maturity. As the child grows into adulthood, new experiences and new relationships can also modify the essence of that first relationship so that again, there may be a shift in behaviour and attitudes to both the self and others. Nevertheless, that first neural footprint leaves an indelible outline on the mind and heart of the individual. It is an outline which continues to provide the shape of reactions and responses, especially at those times in life when circumstances contain the particular elements of emotional threat which have specific meaning to the individual.

As indicated in the opening chapter of this book, my early experiences of great uncertainty led to a fear of abandonment and also of failure as a human being. If we recall the tendency of very young children to perceive their experiences very much from themselves at the centre, the inconsistent care I experienced was interpreted as being due to my 'badness' – an interpretation that was only realigned in late adulthood. This realignment in perception led to a shift in the way relationships were perceived and conducted, and I was fortunate enough to become an 'earned secure' through the consistent love and care of my husband. Nevertheless, it is still possible for me to stub a psychological toe against the outline of that neural imprint causing pain no matter how briefly.

Looking back over my childhood and schooldays – and there are very few clear memories – a general state of anxiety pervaded everything, colouring the type and quality of any friendships accompanied by a desperate need for approval. My strategy was one of extreme compliance, avoidance of confrontation and anxiety to please – one that is certainly not unusual.

My reason for laying some of these personal difficulties before you is a powerful desire to support understanding that for all of us behaviour in the home, in preschool, in school, at work is pervaded by early influences and the impact of work with children and families is bi-directional. The emotional world of the adult influences the child, and the child's emotional world will impact on the adult. Each, therefore, draws a response from the other, and dependent on the type of relationship will subtly or more floridly alter the perception of experience. Our emotional worlds often help to create the atmosphere of an interaction because our initial experiences – that footprint – will influence our expectations of how others will react towards us. We are drawn, often unconsciously, to people who reflect our view of the world, whose experiences have a qualitative similarity to our own whether positive or negative. As Lewis et al. (2000) note, we do not fall in love with everyone we like, nor do we become friends with everyone we meet. Instead, we find characteristics in others which resonate within us, and so across a spectrum of communication and emotional empathy we become drawn to some, more distant with others and perhaps even hostile to a few. In our professional as well as our personal lives, this process will be at work.

This means that for each individual, some children and some parents will prove much easier to be with, no matter what their problems, while another child and their family, even in similar circumstances, will be found difficult and challenging. The child, too, will be drawn to some adults and not others, and this in turn will cause an emotional reaction and behavioural response in the adults concerned. For the adult, how they are able to tolerate a child's apparent rejection of them will depend on what rejection means for them. The emotionally secure adult may feel a little sad or disappointed but will be able to understand that the child has simply shown a preference and can relate the reality of such choices to his or her own life and choice of friends. For the adult who has remained insecure, some may find themselves feeling cold towards the child or appearing indifferent, while others may refuse to accept the child's attitude and constantly try to engage with him or her – but for *their* needs and not the child's particular benefit. If we recall the previous chapters, in order to be able to inhibit our reactions to unpleasant feelings we need to have learnt that they are tolerable and can be resolved, and if not that they must be ignored/subdued or that we must continue to 'call' for reassurance.

The reality of the emotional needs in adults cannot be underestimated, especially in work which involves *relationships* with children and families. Social workers, health visitors and other allied professionals, such as occupational therapists, speech therapists, educational psychologists and so on, all will have occasion to work with children and families and need to be able to establish a relationship with them in order to carry out their responsibilities. Of course, the level, intensity and duration of contact in these professions will vary dependent on the particular type of intervention, but in some situations intense contact will mean that not only is good communication essential but also a level of trust and common understanding between all the participants.

In complex and demanding situations, the toll on the emotional world of such practitioners can be very high. If not acknowledged, such a situation can lead to errors of judgment as they try to deal with the maelstrom of emotions engendered by a particular family, relationship dynamics, and the requirements of the professional role with its targets and paperwork. What a particular practitioner *feels* about the situation will affect their ability to *think* about it.

For example, in the Lord Laming (2003) report into the Victoria Climbié tragedy, he speculated that 'medical staff felt especially uncomfortable about investigating evidence of deliberate harm to children.' While the full report does identify severe organizational failures, it also notes the impact of 'failing relationships' between different professionals and the way in which Victoria's needs were somehow subsumed into the housing needs of the family. It also became evident that individuals did have concerns but these were not recorded at the time, and again it would beg the question why not? Were the adults afraid of being thought foolish or told themselves that what they saw was unimportant? The fundamental response to threat is fight, flight or freeze, and these responses possibly indicate a flight from painful feelings. For some people such feelings are threatening to the deep core of the *self* at an unconscious level because they may resonate with all or part of their own experiences of distress. This then activates those well-worn ancient neural pathways which are then rationalized and explained. This tragedy resurfaced in the recent case of Baby Peter, where the DCSF (2009) review, again headed by Lord Laming, seemed to find similar themes regarding the breakdown of communication between services and in the relationship with the family.

These high-profile tragedies bring into sharp relief the realities of working with children and families and the importance of relationships both with the family and between professionals. For teachers and early years practitioners, contact with children and their families may not normally have the same complexity and intensity as the work of social workers and/or the highly focused intervention that can be provided by health visitors. However, the need for a trusting caring relationship remains as paramount. What is different for these professionals is that they have frequent and sustained contact with children from a range of backgrounds and experiences. For early years practitioners, contact may be not only daily for extended periods of time, but also with the very youngest children. For example, I have encountered practitioners who have cared for babies entering full day care between six to twelve weeks of age. If we recall the intensity and possible necessity of the one-to-one relationship in these early weeks, it begs the question as to how a practitioner can fulfil these needs to the same extent when working in a group care setting. Early years practitioners have a huge, and largely unrecognized, responsibility towards the children in their care, not only because of the high levels of contact but also because they are working with children who are soaking-in the quality of their experiences. The behaviour of these children will reflect how well or otherwise they are able to adapt to the different situations in which they find themselves and the expectations of a range of adults. Their behaviour will also reflect the quality of the relationship each has with these adults, and how they observe the adults behaving towards each other, parents and the other children.

Do what I do

We have seen from the previous chapters the profound impact of early relationships on the child, the influence of shifts in skills and abilities and how these can also influence a child's behaviour as they develop in cognitive abilities, greater mobility and use of verbal language. Throughout all this growth and change there remains the emotional 'loading' of all experiences, and it remains as important for the toddler and young child as it is for the baby that adults continue to monitor and adapt to changing emotional needs.

As we saw in Chapter 3, the ability to regulate or manage emotions begins in infancy with the parents' responses to the child's needs, and Karr-Morse and Wiley (1997) have identified what they consider to be four aspects to such emotional regulation of particular importance to young children: joyfulness, anger, fear and emotional sensitivity. They note that joyfulness is 'crucial to self esteem' and while they also consider that anger and fear may have some genetic, i.e. inherited bias, both can be 'modulated by care giving behaviour'. In other words, a child who seems rather irritable can have this irritability modified by parents who recognize this tendency and find ways to help the child cope. Similarly, a rather fearful, easily startled child can also be supported to feel more confident by sensitive care giving. If such regulation does not occur, the irritable, rather angry infant can become the irritable, angry child who displays high levels of aggression. As Karr-Morse and Wiley point out, by the time such children reach school they may already be labelled troublemakers or bullies. The fearful child in their turn will see danger around every corner if not supported at a pace they can tolerate.

Empathy or sympathy towards someone else can only be learned by the child being shown empathy/sympathy towards their own needs when they are at their most vulnerable, i.e. in infancy and very early childhood. Parents and other carers can also model how the child's actions might impact on others as appropriate by saying that something hurt or someone feels sad if left out of a game, for example. Adults can also model awareness of how their own actions impact on others. Much of the cruelty perpetuated towards animals, other vulnerable children or vulnerable adults is carried out by those who can only recognize their own reactions to their experiences and do not appear to think beyond the confines of their own body. If we remember the example in Chapter 1 of the response to a woman who told some young boys to be quiet, we can see a total lack of awareness or consideration of consequences to actions to *someone else*. However, these boys were very aware of their own feelings in reaction to the woman's actions and so wanted to punish her. The particular instigator of the response obviously could not tolerate what he felt and many professionals working in early years and those teachers working in primary and secondary schools will also have come across children and young people who are equally unable to tolerate frustration, criticism (no matter how kindly meant or positively given) or rejection. Adults too, of course, can remain stuck in this emotional wasteland where they never grow up beyond a very early stage in their emotional development.

Attachment needs

While adults working with children certainly cannot – and should not – classify the quality of a child's attachment relationships, it is still important that the reality of its fundamental nature in influencing a child's behaviour is recognized. As outlined in Chapters 2 and 3, the attachment relationship contributes to the child's feelings of emotional safety and security, impacting on their feelings of self-worth and self-esteem. Such feelings suffuse into a child's attitudes towards exploration, approach and levels of curiosity, but at different levels within any one child. This is because the impact of their attachment relationships will be influenced by the other experiences in their lives, such as aspects of the child's temperament and adult attitudes towards different characteristics.

For example, a child may have an insecure attachment to one or both parents, but may also have experienced warmth and genuine liking from a neighbour who finds the child's character appealing. Such an experience can help balance the child's view of themselves and so the child may have more emotional courage and therefore be able to participate in activities more freely than perhaps expected. Children with mainly secure attachment patterns will also not present 'all of a piece'. A secure child with a shy, quiet temperament will most likely have positive self-belief but may prefer to work alone some of the time, dislike group activities and perhaps have just one particular friend. Such a child may be interpreted by some practitioners as having poor social skills when, in reality, it is simply part of who the child *is*.

However, what is fundamentally crucial for adults/practitioners to understand is that children will have powerful needs for safety, security and reassurance in the absence of their parents when in day care and later school. Furthermore, it is equally important to have awareness that the patterns of behaviour formed by the initial relationship with the parents will dictate the child's style of interaction. Recognition of a child's need for a consistent person who has the child as their primary focus has been the driving force behind the development of the 'key person approach' in early years settings. This concept was initially introduced by Elinor Goldschmied, described in Goldschmied and Jackson (1999) and further developed with Peter Elfer and Dorothy Selleck (Elfer et al., 2003). The key person is intended to provide an alternative source of comfort and reassurance for the child so that they are then able to take advantage of the opportunities provided in the setting. Key persons are intended to have the care of a very small group of children, and the combined approach means that settings become relationship-led rather than task-led (Read, 2010). Of course, in group care individual attention is always going to be more difficult, and Goldschmied also advocated 'islands of intimacy' during the day when children have a specific opportunity to be with their special person.

This, of course, does reflect real life as no parent can spend every hour with their child and indeed it would be unhelpful to do so – children do have to have a degree of independence and space for themselves. However, it is the *reliable and consistent* existence of the *opportunity* for loving care, acceptance and reassurance that allows the feelings of security to develop. Read (2010) reinforces what Elfer et al. (2003) also discuss, i.e. that there is a difference between a key *person* and a key *worker*. The latter tends to be someone who has a set of administrative responsibilities for a small group of children, but in the key person approach the 'role that comes to the foreground is that of the importance of being in a relationship with children set against a background of administrative tasks' (p.64). The focus of responsibility is clearly different – and crucial.

Awareness of the attachment patterns in children is not only important for those working in early years settings but once children start school (which seems to be earlier and earlier), teachers too have to be cognizant of the attachment/emotional needs of children. What teachers in primary schools (and I strongly suspect in secondary schools too) may not fully appreciate is that they become the attachment figure for the child – especially, as Geddes (2006) suggests, for the more anxious child. If there is a class teacher, that person, almost by default, is the consistent, reliable figure and so becomes imbued with the emotional needs of the individuals in the class which, of course, will vary from child to child. Geddes reminds us just how confusing – and big – schools can be, especially in a transition from nursery to school, but of course it does not stop there. Children of any age can find in some aspects of school work, from reading out loud to taking part in any physical exercise, a fear of failure, or simply being able to focus and attend as very difficult. Their innate responses – just as in adults – of fight, flight or freeze will begin to bubble to the surface in any situation they find stressful. The strategies they have learned to cope with these uncomfortable feelings will then come into play, whatever they are. It is the teacher's awareness – just as with early years practitioners – that will allow them to think about what the child may be feeling and to consider what may be a supportive strategy. Awareness and understanding are so important because adults will translate the child's behaviour in a nanosecond through the medium of their own emotional world, attitudes and beliefs, resulting in the specific response to the child at that moment, which may or may not be in tune with the needs of the child.

Geddes also points out that just as the child slowly becomes less reliant on the parent as they grow older, so the child in school gradually becomes more able to learn for themselves but this is, of course, reliant on the relationship with the teacher(s) involved. I wonder how many people remember being put off a subject or even school itself by the attitudes of a particular teacher, and/or whether they felt that school as an entity was safe for them? If school is a place to be feared because of an indifferent ethos – bullying that is not appropriately dealt with or simply a place where no one seems to notice the child who is struggling – then a whole swathe of experience becomes embedded within the psyche of the individual, further sculpting those neural pathways laid down in the earliest years.

Separations and settling

Most adults, whether as parents or professionals working with children and families, recognize that separations are particularly painful for children, and the ability to settle into a new setting can take some children many weeks, even months. In my experience, there can occasionally be a tendency for some practitioners to find those children who seem very unsettled for long periods of time as 'spoilt' or 'babyish' without appreciating that the experiences the child has already had will influence how they view being placed in a strange situation. After all, children have no say in where they go and who they meet for the vast majority of the time. While in many ways this is appropriate in the sense that they cannot yet judge contexts and people, nevertheless it needs to be appreciated just how hard it must be to come to terms with a new environment. Insecure children will also have the added difficulties of their particular world view. Anxious children may find it particularly hard, torn between a desire for comfort and a need to control so that they can have a sense of agency within the turmoil of their uncertainty. As both Gerhardt (2004) and Crittenden (2007, 2005, 1999) describe, these children have learned to monitor their parent(s) closely to bring their attention to them, and so will often try to do the same to the early years practitioner or teacher through helplessness, crying and frequent calls for assistance or reassurance. However, the anxiety may also spill over into hostility both in the home and in the setting. Practitioners will also need to understand that in such households, the care for the child is inconsistent and so might the relationship with the practitioner be equally something of a roller-coaster.

The key aspect of the child's behaviour will be one of anxiety, however expressed, and so the role of the adult is to find ways in which anxiety and tension can be reduced. While it is very demanding for many early years workers and teachers, especially if they have large groups to work with, nevertheless consideration when planning to allow for time for children to settle will be very helpful in the long run. The difficulty and the skill lies in variation of responses as settling for some children will mean time to run, swing, jump, while for others it will be a time to do a puzzle, sit with a book or time just to be with friends. This time need not be long, but perhaps all children would benefit from a 'free choice time' at the beginning of each day which is also age appropriate, consistent and imbued with a warmth that is generated through the initial welcome.

Children who have developed a more avoidant pattern of attachment can appear independent and self-reliant – something that is generally seen approvingly. However, the sensitive adult will notice that the child may not seek help and may seem to avoid contact, similarly to the way the child may emotionally and/or physically avoid being close to the parent. These children may find that an activity or task may be a safe way of interacting with others and it is interesting that boys, who are over-represented in the diagnosis of autism, seem to prefer to get to know one another through a game, a task, a joint interest or rough and tumble. Avoidant children are usually children who have been rejected emotionally as well as possibly being illtreated physically, and it may be helpful to recall the 'still face procedure' discussed in Chapter 3. If we think about the different reactions from boys and girls to the apparent withdrawal of engagement by their mother, we can link this to the types of behaviour that may be seen in the nursery/preschool or classroom. Boys are often the ones who seem to act out their frustrations, and so the boys with the experience of rejection through emotional neglect may appear indifferent to the adult but their behaviour may tell another and very different story.

Loss and grief

Sadly, although thankfully relatively rare, children do suffer the death of a parent, which is traumatic whatever the age of the child. However, there are circumstances which increase the chance of a death occurring, such as a parent who is away fighting in Afghanistan. In addition, road deaths, murder or suicide are tragically also part of this scenario. The particular circumstance of the death will affect the emotional availability of adults as well as their attitudes towards the family, which in turn will influence the child, or children, and affect how they may be supported. In these circumstances the adult professional may play a key part in helping to support both the child and the family. Understanding of the different ways that children may behave at different ages is important. A myth is that very young children get over a death quite quickly, but in reality their periods of apparent preoccupation with other things represent a safety net in the mind as these young children cannot tolerate high levels of grief for long and need to have some respite. Such periods of recovery are often followed by the child being subsumed again in their experience of loss (Lieberman et al., 2003). It is possible that this myth is perpetuated because it is so painful for adults to realize the reality of the very real suffering of a child following the loss of a parent. Of course, circumstances will influence the degree of emotional pain, such as the quality and depth of the relationship and what inner resources the child already has, for example a secure attachment and/or supported from other loved and trusted adults.

In today's society there are so many relationship breakdowns that some children have to endure the loss of a parent which may seem to be just as permanent as an actual death if access is denied or withdrawn. Professionals working with children and families, whatever their role, will encounter and have to support the child whose parents are going through a separation or divorce. For some teachers, there may be more than one child from the same family in their care or with another colleague, and so a combined approach to understanding the differing needs of each child will be important. Children also have to contend with the presence of a new step-parent and possibly step-siblings, and then a new brother or sister, as well as moving from one house to another if shared care or on access visits. If we think about our own attitudes to our home and what becomes precious about it, I wonder if we fully appreciate what an upheaval it might be for children who have to shuttle between places and who then come to nursery or school and misbehave?

The loss of a parent for whatever reason means that the child has to come to terms with the absence of that parent and, unfortunately for the child, the remaining parent is often caught up in the trauma of what has happened and may have little emotional room to comfort and console the child. While taking account of the variations in reactions in individual children – just as adults vary in their reactions to loss and grief – the general pattern of response includes cycles of 'intense distress, emotional withdrawal, anger, emotional detachment' (Lieberman et al., 2003). The concept of cycles of such responses is a helpful one as people, including children, rarely go through the classic phases of grief[1] in a steady progression. Instead they go through the various phases until acceptance is reached and they find the ability to pick up the threads of life again.

Early years practitioners and teachers need to be aware of these cycles and the acute sensitivities of children who, for example, may become extremely upset if they do something wrong. Children in the three to four age range may see themselves as somehow causing the death, or feeling that if they had been good then mummy or daddy would not have gone away. Such feelings are echoed in the circumstance of divorce and separation as the child may also think that they have contributed to their mother or father leaving them. Preschool children who have suffered a bereavement or separation may also think that the situation can be reversed, and this can be very difficult for professionals involved in the family in trying to support the child as well as being sensitive to the realities of any particular situation. Many professionals are going to feel at a loss in such situations and even more so if the bereavement is due to homicide or suicide, or if the particular divorce/separation is very bitter. The child remains vulnerable and distressed and sometimes lonely if the adults involved are focused on their own pain. This is when professionals need to recognize that they themselves may need help and support from grief and bereavement counsellors.

Another situation that many adults may encounter and which will be very demanding of their role is if they encounter children in foster care or who have recently been adopted. Children who are refugees and traveller children are also amongst those who may have experienced considerable change, and refugee children probably have had highly traumatic experiences.

What can help in these situations may seem very basic in many ways, but an understanding of typical child development allows the patterns of behaviour that the child displays to be seen in a context which supports reflection on the child's actual levels of maturation. It can provide a marker for what the child could be achieving and what they are achieving. Understanding the influence of the child's needs for safety and security will also allow practitioners to realize that this must be in place before any kind of formal learning can take place. This is not to say that children will not find certain activities helpful but rather that the activities are used to encourage safe interaction, and also to encourage a sense of mastery and achievement. For children who have been totally at the mercy of adult actions, this can not only be a powerful aid to their self-esteem but also a balm to their troubled hearts and minds.

The other essential is for practitioners to recognize not only their own emotional responses but also a realistic appraisal of their own strengths and limitations. We cannot always deal with everything, and this does not mean that somehow this is failure. Having the humility to accept that a situation may be out of our depth is often the most helpful thing we can do, because then we can go and seek additional help and resources.

I now want to broaden this discussion and think about children's more general fears as these are also times when children's attachment needs and related patterns of behaviour are more likely to come to the fore.

Something strange where danger lurks

What constitutes a threat or danger to a child? As adults we need to remember that what can feel completely ordinary and safe to us can appear threatening in some way to a child. So first we need to consider what the situations are in which a child might be wary. Of course, not all children will find the same situations worrying, as dependent on their temperament and experiences they will have a greater or lesser tendency to approach or withdraw, to be curious or cautious. Therefore, as adults we need to observe the cues that the child might be giving to let us know how they are approaching a particular situation.

If we think back to Chapter 2, we are reminded that we enter this world with an innate reaction to fear/threat via the 'startle reflex'. As babies get older this reaction can become more specific, as we recall that at seven months babies begin to show stranger anxiety, but they can also begin to show wariness or fear to masks and jack-in-the-boxes. This is probably because there is a process occurring within the brain during this time that is refining the processing of human, upright faces and so masks and clown type faces may be disturbing as they do not appear to fit into this growing understanding of *features* as well as expression. Separation anxiety itself as we know can continue in some form right through the lifespan but peaks in children around eighteen to twenty-four months, which is incidentally when many children enter a nursery setting. How such transitions are handled is always important, but perhaps particularly so during this phase. Such fears in preschool children can be increased by house moves and even staying with relatives overnight, again something that can be seen as entirely non-threatening to the adults concerned.

Toddlers around twenty-four months often have fears of the toilet or baths and are afraid that they will vanish down the toilet or down the plug hole. These fears are very real, and some children can become quite distraught at this time. If we consider that this is when toilet training is also beginning, awareness by adults of such fears can help the child be soothed and reassured rather than being thought simply silly or naughty. Children of this age do know something about size and shape, but not enough to realize they can't get go down these tiny spaces.

Practitioners need to be aware of the type of play that is often going on during this period, which is often all about climbing, clambering and going through small spaces such as play tunnels. This type of play helps the child establish their body shape and size. These fears also emerge not long after the child has experienced mirror recognition and identification of body parts, and so all these factors link together helping the child realize that they have a body, it is theirs, but also what type of body it is.

Toilet training can also bring fears of adult reaction to 'accidents', which can profoundly influence a child's later attitude towards using the toilet and can persist into adulthood. I wonder how many people don't like using public toilets, become constipated when on holiday, or are horrified by the idea of using a bedpan or commode in a hospital ward and find it very hard to 'go'?[2] In other words, our feelings affect our bodily functions. Other fears that tend to emerge around this time are of loud noises, fast approaching objects, and often doctors who become associated with unpleasant and possibly painful experiences.

From this age of twenty-four months, children's imagination is also growing in both strength and complexity, and children aged between thirty-six and forty-eight months have a widening range of fearful experiences. They frequently don't like the dark, scary noises (not just loud ones), animals and being left alone. Things like vacuum cleaners and even hairdryers can suddenly seem very frightening. Children's 'concrete thinking' can also add to the fear. For example, a child told that she is going to have her hair cut may suddenly appear terrified. This can be because of a greater understanding of the word 'cut', which can equal 'pain', such as having 'cut one's knee'. Children don't know their hair has no pain sensors (unlike the scalp),so won't know that having a haircut doesn't hurt, but children may fear that it will.

Some children's fear of animals will manifest into a fear of dogs and it is very important that a balance is struck between encouraging caution and avoiding fear. While young children should never be left unsupervised with an animal, it is also important that they learn how to react around animals, not to hurt and tease them and how to pat and stroke appropriately. Dogs can be great friends for children and can help them in many ways to gain confidence, but sensible caution is always necessary. Just like very small children, an animal cannot gauge the motivation behind behaviour – it only knows what it feels.

Another very strong fear for preschoolers is fear of the dark, and is one that takes the longest to disappear and may persist throughout adulthood.

Even everyday situations can frighten some children – going to bed can become a frightening time. This may be because children are becoming more aware of 'falling asleep', and this combined with being in the dark and possibly alone in the bed can combine to transform this into something potentially fearful. Their greater imaginations can also be at work, seeing shadows at the top of stairs or fearing a shape under the bed. Children can have nightmares at this age too. Adults need to remember that children in this age range still have difficulty separating out what might be fantasy and what is reality. For example, children who were told a story about a monster in a box (who turned out to be a very small and friendly creature) had a box as a prop. Afterwards, even though they knew the box was empty and it was only a story, there was still some wariness when approaching the box.

School-aged children generally have fears that adults may relate to more clearly, such as storms, fire or injury, but they can worry about these things greatly. Children can also be distraught over news items, for example about climate change, war, attacks in the home and burglaries. It is absolutely beholden to adults to ensure that information the child sees or listens to is within their cognitive capabilities. Children of this age are not very able to assess the likelihood of any particular occurrence; it is not until they get older that they begin to realize that these things don't happen that often or are far away or not happening in the present and can readjust their levels of fear.

They also worry about the state of the relationship between their parents and are more consciously aware of problems, which can then spill over into anxieties at school. They can also become very worried about what they generally see on television and the Internet, and so practitioners need to think about what a child might be watching at home that could cause variations in behaviour or be the cause of anxious questioning. Children might also be exposed to age-inappropriate video games or films because of a lack of parental monitoring or older siblings, and these can also affect the behaviour of younger children as they may act out what they have seen and might have excited and/or disturbed them.

The role for adults with children's fears are not to minimize them or make the child feel stupid or silly, but while taking these fears seriously must guard against making too much of them. If the child expresses great fear too, this could lead to a child feeling that such fears are insurmountable. Children look to adults for the means to provide boundaries for their fear so that they can find their courage and learn to face their anxieties. This has to be done gently and at the pace the child can tolerate, and so ultimately the child can learn not only how to approach the terrifying spider but also to realize that they can face some of the inside fears as well.

So far in this chapter, we have thought about the situations that can cause children to be anxious and fearful. This next section moves on to thinking about the factors that can influence the way in which an adult interprets the behaviour of a child, because it is the *interpretation* that will guide the adult response.

Interpreting behaviour

What constitutes acceptable and unacceptable behaviour? How do we decide if the behaviour we witness is a problem or perhaps part and parcel of the child growing up as we saw in Chapter 4? As discussed in Chapters 3 and 4, children will develop strategies and patterns of behaviour in response to their experiences, and so will we. So as adults we need to reflect on what is our attitude to the crying child, the angry, disruptive child or the child who appears to whine and cling? A clue to our own emotional world lies in how we think about our friends and their problems and our approach to our own problems. Do we feel that they and we should 'get on with it', 'pull ourselves together', or perhaps it is necessary to 'put on a brave face', or do we ruminate for days if not weeks about something someone has said or done? What emotions do we find more 'comfortable', and what emotions do we freely express and which might we 'keep under wraps'? Do we find happiness threatening? This may seem a strange thing to say, but some people are afraid of happiness because on some level, they always fear that something is bound to go wrong. This applies to children too who can be fearful of feeling happy if, in their short life, they have already encountered far too many disappointments or have been let down by adults too often. Such an attitude will colour their responses to all the delightful things you want to plan for them.

Interpreting a child's behaviour may also be influenced by our particular educational levels, cultural and social expectations. Also as professionals working with children and families, could a particular professional perspective influence the way in which a child's behaviour is interpreted? Ben-Sasson et al. (2007) found, in their study of occupational therapists and psychologists, that different professionals varied in their assessment as to whether a child's behaviour was due to anxiety or sensory over-responsivity. In other words, their particular professional training and context influenced the way they each interpreted their observations. The problem is that professional bias may not only influence an individual's responses but also the type of interventions that might be undertaken. Awareness of the particular focus of training needs to be recognized so that a more holistic approach can be taken. For example, in the study quoted above, both sets of professionals could have had a correct interpretation but each was only providing part of the jigsaw, i.e. the child's behaviour was an *amalgam* of sensory over-responsivity and anxiety. After all, the child will have had an emotional reaction to their sensory sensitivity and each will have 'fed' the other, leading to a distressed and/or angry and/or fearful child.

In the introduction to the Crittenden and Claussen book (2000), Crittenden provides a very sad and salutary example of how a group of researchers allowed their professional distance to influence their thoughts about a child. She describes the behaviour of a four-year-old boy who 'seemed extremely independent and distant from an intimidating withdrawn mother who exuded hostility' during a Strange Situation study. When left alone by his mother this seemingly independent little boy 'fell apart' and ultimately curled up in a foetal position emitting 'eerie wails'. To condense the example, the researchers when assessing the situation thought that he was probably a type C (anxious insecure) child, and when asked by Crittenden how they thought the boy felt 'they said he began with genuine distress but ended up pretending to cry' and that he had probably 'feigned helplessness in order to coerce adults into taking care of him'.

Crittenden's astonishment at this judgement was superseded by her astonishment at no-one apparently being able to recognize his 'unspeakable agony as being beyond tears or thought that he needed or deserved to be held comfortingly, even if only by a stranger' (p.9). The 'stranger', incidentally, had tried to 'jolly him along', saying that he was a big boy and 'you are not really crying, you don't even have tears'. It was only after Crittenden had spoken about her feelings regarding this boy that she was further astonished that the researchers – including the person who had been the 'stranger' in the study – all agreed with her and were 'openly relieved to discover that they were permitted to feel for him'. She ends this example by asking 'Where do scientists put their feelings when they work? Where should we put them?'

I would add that it is not only scientists/researchers who may not permit themselves to feel for a child and maybe for their parents. Perhaps, as in this case, it would be almost unbearable to do so as the emotional suffering of this little boy was very great. Incidentally, he also provided a poignant example of how much a child will want their mother in times of distress even when she has shown herself to be virtually unavailable. Adults may see their role – as these researchers plainly did – as somehow being divorced from the situation, to be objective rather than subjective. Of course, there is a paradox here, because professionals have to have a degree of objectivity and distance in order for them to see a situation clearly and be able to function when faced with distressing and/or complex situations.

However, this objectivity does not mean dismissing the emotional impact of the work but instead being very aware of it. It is then that ways in which to channel the empathy or sympathy and feelings of distress into positive ways of providing support can be thought about. The researchers in Crittenden's example certainly would not have been helping this child because of their efforts to be objective. In fact, their judgement was punitive in its tone, and one wonders what form interventions would have taken without Crittenden's own intervention and compassionate challenge. Such a situation can happen to professionals in any field. The absorbed distress is unwanted – and painful – and therefore a defence mechanism of fight, for example, against these uncomfortable feelings can translate into anger against the child, the family, the situation, the case load, the numbers in the class and so on.

As well as the professional lens, there are other factors that can add to the mix of influences towards interpretation. For example a child's general manner, their use of eye contact, manner of speech and approach, even the clothes the child might be wearing and their overall appearance. In exactly the same way, parents will be influenced by their emotional, social, educational and cultural history in how they perceive the professional – and vice versa.

What all professionals need to think about when considering their role with children applies equally to working with parents. Currently there is a great deal of pressure on early years practitioners and teachers to work with parents, but this is not an academic exercise. It involves human beings relating to other human beings, with all the issues that can arise both within and between us all. Before anyone can help a child develop their potential and/or support, a parent become more secure and confident with their children, there has to be awareness of the particular professional, educational, social and cultural lens through which we examine all those relationships.

Looking through the gender lens – expectations and interpretations

This section is imbued with political incorrectness as I want to talk about differences between the genders rather than reinforce the idea that the genders are interchangeable and a 'one size fits all' approach. Of course, I am far from alone in acknowledging that boys and girls are different in the way they can behave, react and respond and of course there are multiple similarities. However, while the differences may be subtle they do exist and can influence the attitudes and responses of those in early years settings and schools. It is particularly important for such recognition as the workforce in early years and primary schools is overwhelmingly female and it is not until secondary school that there is more of a balance between genders. This means that many boys, especially because of relationship breakdowns, are without sound, solid male role models who provide them with a picture of just how good men can be. Currently men in general have been somewhat sidelined, with their role as fathers and mentors being perceived – albeit only by some – as relatively unimportant. However, there is a sea change occurring and I find it extremely poignant that there are many initiatives in Britain both at government and local level to try to draw men back into nurseries, pre-schools and schools to become involved again with their own and other's children.[3]

What has been particularly unhelpful has been the idea of gender equality, which has led to some perceiving that male and female behaviour is somehow completely interchangeable and that the only differences are social and cultural. While certainly not denying that social expectations and cultural expectations can play a very important part in shaping behaviour, nonetheless the issue that needs to be asserted is that neither gender has any type of superiority but instead that the genders bring different but complementary skills to human life. Furthermore, much of the innate behaviours in either gender have evolutionary roots and the fact that women have the babies means that many of the skills and abilities females have are linked to this profound event. For example, it is well known that females have greater sensitivity to reading facial expressions and eye gaze, and we saw already in Chapter 3 the importance of 'motherese'. Such skills are crucial for infants and so may have been enhanced in women as an evolutionary necessity. Men's proficiency in visual-spatial skills may also have its roots in our hunter-gatherer history.

Such differences begin before birth with a huge surge in testosterone (and other hormones) during foetal growth between seven to sixteen weeks, and variations in testosterone during this phase can influence the development of the boy's sexual organs *and* the brain. Just after birth, male babies have another surge in testosterone levels, which peaks at around two months and then settles to about the same level as girls at around six months. If we recall, this approximately corresponds with the timing of the intense relationship babies have with their mothers and then the emergence at around four months of a wider interest in play items and the general environment. The next huge surge in testosterone is unsurprisingly at puberty, ranging anywhere from ages eleven to thirteen, and the increase can be as much as 800 per cent (McClure, 2008) – no wonder boys can be just as irrational and topsy-turvy in their emotions as girls! McClure provides a very helpful analogy, that girls and women experience a flavour of this surge every month prior to menstruation. This is when oestrogen and testosterone levels in women alter, with oestrogen dropping and the testosterone becoming more obvious in its effects. However, teenage boys are experiencing the effects of this surge every day.

McClure is especially insightful in considering the general cycles of testosterone in boys and how this can influence their behaviour. As women, we seem to be much more prepared to allow some leeway for the chemical/hormonal changes in teenage girls for example, but seem less so when considering the needs of boys. An especially interesting factor is that boys' testosterone levels appear to go in two-hourly cycles during the day, and if we link this to how levels may also rise when playing in a group, then we can understand a little more why boys may appear to be more or less attentive at different times of the day. Another piece of this testosterone jigsaw is that levels overall tend to rise (in temperate climates) in late summer and in the autumn, and of course this is just when academic terms are ending and beginning. Therefore boys' behaviour may not only reflect the particular circumstances surrounding finishing or starting school (or nursery) but also the fact that they may be a little more 'scratchy' and hyper anyway. Boys will obviously vary as individuals in both the levels of testosterone and its effects – just as not all girls react in the same way premenstrually – but it is certainly an issue that might help practitioners think about the boys more compassionately. Other factors that raise testosterone is anger and aggression *in others* as well as in the self, which explains why a calm approach from parents and practitioners can be so helpful in reducing tension, while meeting anger with anger can escalate the problem.

Perhaps the most crucial aspect of the effects of testosterone is the effect it has on helping to shape brain 'wiring'. The surge in the foetus and postnatally are all helping to influence how the neural footprint of the male baby's experiences via the workings of this powerful hormone to help the child become the man. Although it is obviously only part of the chemical/hormonal activity in the brain, nevertheless it contributes to the way in which boys and men tend to feel and think about the world. No two human brains are wired identically as we know, but all human brains carry with them the same genetic messages for the unfolding of structures, maturational levels, hormonal and chemical activity, sculpted by experience and within the parameters of whether the growing child is a girl or a boy. Levels of hormonal activity will also be modified by experiences and the picture is a highly complex one, but this does not eliminate the reality that perception and learning styles between boys and girls are different. Another caveat is that within genders there will also be variations of behaviour styles and patterns, but again, sometimes we do need to think in generalizations to help us understand the wider picture – we do need to see the wood as well as the trees.

A recognition of broadly different learning styles is particularly important when dealing with all ages of children, including the very young age range, as introducing some educational activities before a child is ready can mean that they lose interest and enthusiasm very early – and it is so hard to recapture. Boys' language and literacy skills in particular appear to develop at least six months behind girls, and unfortunately because the *early* achievement of these skills is seen as so important, girls obviously appear to be more successful. This early maturation in girls reflects the different ways that male and female brains tend to be wired, with females generally appearing to have more connectivity between the two hemispheres, whereas boys tend to have stronger connectivity within the right hemisphere. As McClure (2008) says, 'a girl's brain is developing in a way that develops communication, full stop' (p.74). What is dangerous for adults is because girls are often so much better at communication and social skills somehow they are seen as better overall or even superior to boys in some way. Such an attitude can pervade the emotional atmosphere within any setting, and boys are extremely good at picking up subtle displays of preferences in their teachers or other professionals. Boys also tend to show their feelings less but only by around five or six, and in fact Newberger (1999) reported on a study back in 1984 which noted expressiveness in babies to be greater in boys than girls (when photos were examined by adults). In fact, boys and girls tend to show similar emotions in the preschool years although potentially girls' greater social skills may mean that already they are *perceived* as more emotionally expressive. However, boys and men can *feel* just as strongly as women but express their feelings differently, and here social and cultural mores and traditions come into play.

Sax (2005, 2007) notes that teachers and others need to be aware of the overall preferred learning styles of boys and girls and that each gender is more likely to achieve if adults can adapt their ways of working to accommodate this. He provides a very interesting example (Sax 2005, pp.103–105) where he describes the different ways boys and girls can learn about the Fibonacci series in maths.[4] In the example, both sets of pupils learned about this process but the boys did it via pure numbers while the girls learned via looking at flower petals and so on. This was *not* patronizing to the girls, it was simply taking something that is more appealing to girls generally (i.e. flowers) and using it to explain a concept. Boys generally tend to like numbers for their own sake. They also tend to enjoy discovery, construction, exploring, problem solving but often don't respond well to formal sitting and listening until older.

As well as learning styles, boys and girls also have differences in colour perception, with girls generally being better at identifying subtle shades. There are also hearing differences, with boys responding more easily to directly addressed (without confrontational eye contact) and straightforward instructions. Boys' physical development is also different; at age four boys are still developing their large muscles, while girls are already busy 'connecting up' their fingers and toes and hence find activities such as beading, threading and using pencils easier while the boys generally may find this harder. Again, given today's pressures on early writing and reading, it is noticeable how many boys may be struggling and being seen – and seeing themselves – as failing. McClure (2008) provides an excellent piece of advice regarding the introduction of reading, which she gained from a paediatric physiotherapist, i.e. 'when they can skip, they are ready to read'.

To summarize, it is essential in the race for equal opportunities that professionals do not become bound up in ideologies and forget to look at physiological, biological, neurological and emotional realities in the children in front of them. All children are unique and special, all are individuals, but to deny, as said earlier, that gender is simply a social construction is to do great harm to both boys and girls, as we can become blind to genuine differences in patterns of maturation and behaviour. Subtle they may be, but their consequences if ignored can be profound.

The final section in this chapter looks at some broad principles regarding the provision of an optimal environment for all children when outside the home.

The environment

Children can become very upset when in unfamiliar surroundings, and perhaps we should remember how we too can feel when away from home, and just as we can feel safe and soothed when back home so do children. Being in a strange and/or threatening environment can elicit the need for comfort and reassurance, and wanting to be home denotes the need for the safe place. Who has not heard the child cry 'I want to go home', and how often are we ready to hear the need for reassurance? For example, for us the day-care setting, the childminder's home, the classroom may feel welcoming, but for some children on a first visit the place will be strange, smells, sounds, décor and furnishings are all new and possibly unfamiliar. The space in a day-care setting may be much larger than the child's own rooms at home, which again may seem unsettling. I wonder how many of us have visited a childhood haunt as an adult and found it to be so much smaller than we remember? If not, then think how large places can appear when we are relatively so small. We need to add this awareness to what the child may already be feeling at the separation from their parent, so their grief at parting is compounded by their possible reactions to the actual space in which they find themselves, adding to their fear and to their distress.

What constitutes a caring environment?

There are three aspects to thinking about the environment: the emotional atmosphere, the indoor environment and the outdoor environment. The Oxfordshire County Council/Sure Start team have produced a document called 'My Space'[5] which particularly looks at the environment from the child's point of view, and what was particularly striking were the children's needs for emotional warmth in whatever situation, so we will begin with the emotional atmosphere.

For young children in day care or entering school, the transition from home to a different environment in which they are going to spend some time means that they need to feel safe. An innovative early intervention project entitled 'The Circle of Security'[6] based on attachment theory introduced the concepts of a 'safe base' and a 'safe haven' as key components of secure attachment relationships, and these concepts retain their validity in organizational situations. A child needs a safe haven for their emotions and a safe base for their exploratory and learning needs. Just as with parents, some early years practitioners and teachers will find that dealing with a child's emotional needs is easier than the child's exploratory/learning needs and vice versa. For example, one teacher I met was apparently comfortable supporting and encouraging the children in her class but appeared to find it very difficult in dealing with a child who, aged five years, was already reading well; she insisted that the child followed a particular reading scheme with the other children but this made the child very miserable.

The questions that children asked regarding their emotional space were very moving and included:

- Do you know me, my family, my circumstances?
- Who will I meet here and how do I know who is special to me?

This clearly identified how children want to be seen as individuals and, most importantly, *cared* about. It also highlights the information discussed earlier that early years professionals and teachers do become the alternative attachment figure and a key person for the child. They need to know so that they know where to turn.

Another interesting question asked was, how do people behave in the particular setting? This pulls together the need for connection between the child and the other people and the importance of imitation as a strategy in which they will find out how people behave and fit in. It also identifies how much children need to know what the boundaries are, where they can go and what they are able to do. A lack of clarity in such situations is very unhelpful for most children. Uncertainty breeds anxiety, and children will respond according to their particular strategies.

An important message for everyone is that when *all* children feel relaxed and not stressed through hypersensitivity to sensory information or are feeling confused, anxious, angry or fearful, they are then able to *really hear* what adults are saying to them and therefore respond more appropriately.

The indoor environment

The key questions that children asked regarding their indoor environment include whether the environment was welcoming and inviting. Children also wanted to know whether they could move around freely, have opportunities to be independent, explore and, interestingly, use all their senses. Places to rest, eat and problem solve also seemed to be important. It struck me on reading through this document that much of what children wanted from their environment was very similar to what adults want, which is to feel safe, welcomed and have opportunities to express themselves. Adults, like children, need to feel secure but also competent within whatever context they happen to be. However, as adults we do sometimes have the luxury of adapting or altering our environment to suit our needs and tastes, but children do not often have this opportunity and their environment is the one we adults present to them. This emphasizes just how important it is for us to think about what children need, whatever their age, always remembering what makes us feel at home. While, as always has to be said, what suits one may not suit another, there are still these broad principles that seem to apply to a range of contexts and which adults, whatever their particular professional role, can think about and examine the environment they provide through the eyes of the child.

The outdoor environment

What children seemed to want in this section of the Sure Start report was permission to be outside, and one of the questions was whether adults like to be outside Having witnessed adults standing in a playground, muffled up to the eyebrows, arms tightly folded, I do wonder what message this is giving to the children about outdoor activities. The other aspect, sadly all too often seen especially in schools for older children, is the sterile nature of the outdoor area. Children, on the other hand, had asked for:

• places and features to sit in, on, under, lean against, and provide shelter and shade
• different levels and nooks and crannies, places that offer privacy and views.

I wonder how many playgrounds have seats, shelters, tables as well as the more obvious outdoor equipment? Some nurseries and primary schools do have the most beautiful outside areas, not all large by any means but with resources adapted to the practicalities of the environment. Small seats, growbags, planted-up areas using discarded tyres and so on are all put to good use by imaginative and resourceful practitioners and teachers and are a delight for children, staff and parents.

The principles appear to be that children need to know that adults like being outside too, they need to know what they can do outside, and they need to have places just to be as well as being active and involved.

Summary

In many ways, the role of the adult can be summed up in a simple phrase, 'know the child', as it is only through knowing and thereby understanding that adults can really get behind behaviour and into the 'skin' of the child. Adults cannot get away from the huge responsibility they have towards children, not only to support their growth and potential but also to provide safety, comfort and reassurance. To this end adults also need to know themselves, so that with their own needs and strengths acknowledged and supported they can then turn the spotlight of attention onto the child in their care. We are only young once, and this is the time when that neural footprint is laid down; children need adults who can help form that footprint with compassion, understanding, sympathy, care, knowledge and wisdom.

Chapter 6

Behaviour as the self's mirror

Over the past twenty or so years, there has been an explosion of research into the brain and its workings supported by the development of sophisticated technology such as Positron Emission Tomography (PET)[1] and Magnetic Resonance Imaging/functional Magnetic Resonance Imaging (MRI/fMRI)[2] scans. Such innovations have allowed researchers to see the living brain 'at work', providing great insights into function and maturation even with the reservations that imaging is undertaken in 'artificial' circumstances. Nevertheless, in combination with more traditional forms of research into brain structure and function, such as electroencephalograms (EEGs) which measure the electrical activity of the brain, a much more comprehensive understanding is emerging. This greater understanding of brain function and maturation has served to lend weight to the reality of the impact of experience, especially so in the first years of life. While there may be argument and debate regarding the *nature* of these long-term effects, the fact that there *is* an effect seems to be generally accepted. Teasing out the roots of adult behaviour can be difficult as ongoing experiences and overall brain maturation can add to the complex mix of why someone behaves as they do. Nevertheless, even in studies of dementia, Stokes (2009, p.106) notes 'our earliest years, of which we have little or no memory, are a time rich in promise, but also a time of learning, decisions and discoveries that make us who we are today'. He goes on to say:

> What happens prior to our earliest accessible memories is laid down as personal truth. It is just what we know about ourselves, the way we are. The question is can we forget that which is not remembered? Can we lose that which has not been laid down as an accessible memory trace? The answer is, in all likelihood, no. Hence these early experiences and lessons remain part of who we are, exercising their influence but forever inaccessible.

In Stoke's deeply moving case studies he has found that recognition of patterns of behaviour laid down in the earliest part of life can provide clues for entering into and understanding the world of someone whose behaviour would otherwise appear inexplicable. He also found that behaviour always has a meaning at some level, and this is just as true in the beginnings of our life as it is both during it and towards the end, no matter how it may be expressed by the individual. For the very young, just as with those suffering from dementia or other types of mental illness or those with profound learning disabilities, behaviour is the primary language of communication – a language that needs to be learned by those who are observing, supporting and helping.

Fortunately, in the early years we do have the markers of the broad shifts and changes that occur to help guide our thinking, and the typically developing child will gradually be able to use verbal language to express their thoughts, needs, hopes and dreams, although some will always find words difficult and prefer to act out or use any of the arts in order to connect with others. However, we now know that it is the artful brain that mediates all our experiences and that mediation results in what we do.

The preceding chapters have examined the frameworks suggested for reflecting on the meaning of behaviour. Chapter 2 drew on the greater understanding of brain growth and function, emphasizing the rapid growth and development of the human brain in the first years of life. In particular, the knowledge that the child's reactions to an experience and/or situation that appears threatening to them is embedded in ancient, neurological systems and only with support and help can a child begin to rationalize the validity or otherwise of the danger. Chapter 3 examined in more detail the intricacies of the relationship between child and parent, in particular with the mother. Fathers of course are hugely important, but their role is different and complementary to that of the mother; the male perspective and styles of relating provide another important dimension to the child's experience. Chapter 4 emphasized the ongoing, unfolding of development itself and how simply the passage of time brings with it broadly expected shifts and changes in skills and abilities, with accompanying shifts in both the child's expectations and needs. For the adult, too, the child growing older brings with it new expectations and challenges. Chapter 5 then thought about adults who work with children and families and the particular sensitivities they need to have towards all the differing needs and life experiences of the children in their care. The importance of self-awareness and the adult's own emotional world was also stressed. Through all the chapters, however, there have been two common threads. First, that behaviour, in its essence, is an expression of what we are feeling, how we manage those feelings and the level at which we can think about them. Second, that our earliest experiences lay down a 'neural footprint' profoundly influenced by our relationships with others.

Such relationships are, of course, not the only influences that guide our particular patterns and styles of behaviour. Social and cultural mores, traditions, expectations are all part of a significant network, which guide how adults both interact with and perceive children. Bronfenbrenner's bio-ecological systems theory[3] identifies bidirectional 'layers' of influence on individual development, for example family, religion, school, community, culture, society and global influences, and ultimately brings the focus back to the child at the centre with recognition of the importance of the child's own biological development as a 'primary environment'.

What is a child? A wider view

How we view childhood itself, as a society, does impact on what we expect of children. What we think about childhood and children often has its roots in past perceptions and what we remember about our own childhoods plus what we feel we want children to be. Cunningham (2006) reflects on how some of the main ideas of past centuries are still evident in current society. For example, both the idea of the innocence of childhood and the concept of a right to have a childhood begin in the Industrial Revolution. During this time, the miserable life of children in factories led some philanthropists to promote the idea that children were owed a duty of protection and care by adults.

The biology and general development of children obviously also has an impact on our perceptions, but even this is not static as changes in overall health and diet play a part. For example, as Cunningham (2006) notes, the age at which menstruation starts has reduced overall by about three years in a century because of improved diet and general health, so earlier menstruation will alter attitudes towards how and when childhood ends. What parents and other adults involved with children need, however, is a way of understanding that childhood is a progression – it is a part of life and a stage of preparation. While puberty marks the beginning of the next stage in life's journey, it is not a psychological or physical border where on one side humans behave in a childish way and on the other side they behave like adults. Different behaviours do obviously emerge but they are part of what has gone before, and as any parent with teenagers will know, 'childish' behaviour can still be prevalent while at other times their children can appear to have the wisdom of Solomon.

The age of criminal responsibility in different parts of the world also provides some insight into adult notions about children's capabilities and understanding. In England, Wales and Northern Ireland it is currently ten years (in Scotland it is eight years, although this is being revised), and this is the lowest in Europe where ages are vary between fourteen, fifteen, sixteen and even eighteen years. Attitudes towards the actual crimes committed by children can also highlight adult perceptions of responsibility, especially how such crimes are presented in the media.

For example, the Mary Bell[4] case in 1968 was *relatively* restrained in its reporting and her abusive background was highlighted with apparently a greater understanding of her 'diminished responsibility due to her experiences'. The Jamie Bulger case in 1993, however, was extensively reported and the 'evil' nature of the two boys was a common theme in the newspapers even though their individual backgrounds were also abusive. This seems even more paradoxical given that in 1993, the neuroscience evidence was beginning to emerge and Bowlby's work on attachment was also well established – but perhaps not in the mainstream media. It was after this trial that an ancient principle of *doli incapax* was repealed, which broadly said that children aged between ten and thirteen years could not be criminally responsible unless the prosecution could prove otherwise. Sixteen years after the Bulger trial, little seems to have changed in general attitudes towards children's criminal behaviour. This is in spite of the enormous and increasing amounts of evidence that serve to help us understand that what we do to children in their earliest years matters and profoundly affects the way in which they feel towards themselves and others.

Attitudes to how children are brought up also vary, both across and within generations as well as within different societies. Grille (2008) describes attitudes in pre-war Germany, for example, where 'every child is a battle' was the overriding sentiment.

Child-care manuals in that country at that time advocated 'rigorous obedience training from the earliest time of infancy'. While many parents probably did not follow that advice, nevertheless it represented the prevailing ethos for parenting. In England too, some parenting manuals, notably the advice of John Watson in the 1920s, also advised against too much maternal care and suggested regimented routines. Echoes of such thinking are still prevalent today, and advice regarding strict routines for sleeping and feeding schedules remain very popular.

Such ideas and their particular prevalence in some social groups will influence the emotional well-being of the children to a level which will depend on just how strictly a parent is prepared to follow the advice. For example, I met a new mother in the super-market a few weeks before writing this, and while we were unloading our shopping she told me of her new baby. She also told me she had been bought a number of parenting manuals, one of which advocated these very strict, highly detailed, timed regimes for feeding sleep, play, together with the notion of 'controlled crying'. She laughed while she told me that she was able to carry out the instructions for about a day but became so distraught at leaving her baby to cry that she threw the book in the dustbin and said that she was going to do what she and her husband felt was right. I told her to follow her instincts!

So, in today's society, how do we see children and childhood? In many ways there is more attention paid to the emotional well-being of children, and yet at the same time there is great concern that the society we live in may not be the most positive for children. Caccioppo and Patrick (2008) note that a UNICEF survey of twenty-one wealthy nations found that the United States came in 'second to last in terms of the welfare of children with only the United Kingdom faring worse' (p.247). While their book focuses on the United States, the fact that this country was even worse makes his comments valid for both countries. He feels that the real problem is the emphasis on independence as a desirable state. However, he points out that independence has another side: that of being alone, feeling unconnected with others. True independence means that a person can feel confident in their feelings, thoughts and behaviour as well as having respect for others, their feelings and thoughts.

Other studies, for example several commissioned by the Centre for Social Justice,[5] including *The Next Generation* (which focused on the early years) (2008) and *Every Family Matters* (2009) (an extensive review and recommendations surrounding family law chaired by David Hodson), note that, in spite of the high levels of cohabitation in this country, there seemed to be remain a desire for marriage and stable relationships. The study also found that those questioned did link family breakdown with anti-social behaviour. The Layard and Dunn (2009) report for the Children's Society, *A Good Childhood*, is about children's experiences of childhood. While more generally 'upbeat' it also emphasizes the importance to the children questioned of family life, friend-ship and feeling cared for. Adults in their turn, in this report, often felt that they did not have enough time for their families, with a 'knock on effect' again on family life. The Hosking and Walsh WAVE (2005) report, while focusing on violence, provided extensive research studies to link early development with later manifestations of prob-lems, especially the lack of a nurturing environment in the earliest years. The Adverse

Child Experiences Report (ACE) by Felitti et al. (1998, and 2003 for follow-up) of 17,000 people across three generations identified three particularly significant adverse experiences, i.e. child abuse, family dysfunction and neglect, which appeared to have a profound impact on later health and well-being. Another very influential analysis of knowledge about early human development, edited by Shonkoff and Phillips (2000) in the United States, evaluated research from a wide range of sources in response to their perception of the 'explosion of research in the neurobiological, behavioural and social sciences'. The recommendations from this huge meta-analysis built on four main themes:

1   All children are born wired and ready to learn.
2   Early environments matter and nurturing relationships are essential.
3   Society is changing and the needs of young children are not being addressed.
4   Interactions among early childhood science, policy and practice are problematic and demand dramatic re-thinking. (p.4)

The findings of research and these various reports together with the timely publication of well-researched and received works such as Palmer's (2006) *Toxic Childhood*, Gerhardt's (2004) *Why Love Matters: How affection shapes a baby's brain*, Sunderland's (2006) *The Science of Parenting* and Biddulph's (2006) *Raising Babies*, which were aimed at a wider audience than just academics/practitioners, point to not only a growing recognition of the influence of the early years on subsequent development but also the impact of the child's experiences within their family environment.

While some of the studies mentioned above tend to focus on the effects of trauma such as neglect and abuse with their emotional consequences, the reality that these adverse events have consequences has served to highlight that all early experiences *matter* and that such consequences may linger through the lifespan in either a florid or more subtle manifestation. For example, general, quiet unhappiness or difficulties in relationships, feelings of not being quite good enough, can pervade someone's whole life, leading to a sense of dissatisfaction, of feelings such as 'is this all there is?'

Material wealth is not necessarily the answer as people can live very simple lives but feel content – the sense of a self that is valued does come from within, as witnessed by the courage and dignity demonstrated by some people living in the most dire circumstances. For example, when working for a short time in India alongside Dr Jack Preger who ran a street clinic, he had arranged for a woman and her baby to go to the hospital. She lived by the side of one of the pillars beneath Howrah station in Calcutta and when we went along together with the interpreter to collect her to go to the hospital, she asked us to wait a moment. As we watched, she searched amongst her bundle of belongings (very few) and pulled out a piece of material. She then removed the scarf that was around the baby and put on this clean one. She also smoothed herself down, patting her hair and pulling her headscarf more neatly around her head. She was making herself ready to go to the hospital and was ensuring that she and the baby were as presentable as could be. Her dignity and self-respect profoundly moved me, and I shall never forget it. Somehow, somewhere, she had been given the gift of respect which she held and valued and would, no doubt, pass onto her baby.

The realities of the need for a good childhood, the role of parents and therefore the changing role of professionals working with children and families has led to a range of initiatives by the British government, with perhaps the most influential document in recent years, *Every Child Matters: Change for Children* (DfES, 2004), which was a response to the findings by Lord Laming (2003) into the death of Victoria Climbié mentioned in the previous chapter. The Children's Act in the same year (2004) provided the necessary legislation to support the recommended outcomes. Another document produced by the current (Labour) British government is *Think Family* (2007), which also provides a model of the influences on child development and again reflects the shift from thinking about child development in isolation to thinking about what factors impact on such development (p.12).

A further recent innovation has been the formation of a Department for Children, Schools and Families and the appointment of a Children's Commissioner. The British government also set out *The Children's Plan: Building brighter futures* (DCSF, 2007) which aimed to provide a coherent ten-year strategy for how children and families will be supported. Another initiative, *Healthy Lives, Brighter Futures* has also been produced (2009), along with the piloting of an intensive programme of intervention for families deemed to be at risk. This is the Health-Led Parenting Programme based on the Nurse–Family Partnership (NFP) developed by Professor David Olds in the United States. The goal for the English version, entitled *The Family–Nurse Partnership* (FNP) to distinguish it from the US programme, has been set out as ultimately to reduce social exclusion (Hall and Hall, 2007).

There has also been the creation of Children's Trusts and the national provision of Sure Start Children's Centres which were designed to ensure that services for children were in one location (or at least close by). In addition, policies have also focused on the wider provision of day care, which is a reflection of significant change in society with the growing numbers of younger and younger children being placed in day care provision for a variety of reasons, and the trend is for numbers to continue to rise. As a response to this steady rise in numbers of infants and very young children in day care, the Primary National Strategy documentation[6] is stated to have been formulated in order to help practitioners plan care and learning that is right for each child at each stage of their development, ensure earlier identification of particular needs and support a wider integration of services. In addition, from 2011 the teaching of personal, social, health and economic education is proposed to be a *statutory* part of the National Curriculum. Currently, personal, social and health education is broadly offered in primary and secondary schools, but the concern is regarding expectations of teachers and how their training will accommodate this additional dimension to their work.

The key point is not whether as the Layard and Dunn (2009) inquiry suggest, things are generally felt to be not as bad as painted in the media and most children are generally content, but instead the very real issue that *all* sections of society recognize the profound influence of the quality of the care and nurture in the early years. The very fact that the British and US governments have produced so many initiatives suggests that there are genuine concerns, ranging from binge drinking in younger and younger children to a perceived rise in anti-social behaviour, again by younger children.

However, the building of a human being who feels a sense of self-esteem and self-worth cannot just be a 'programme' and/or part of a school curriculum. How to be emotionally healthy and behave in ways that are positive and promote well-being also cannot be imbued into children and young people through lessons alone. This is *not* to say that these are not useful or helpful, but the roots of well-being are developed early and it is the work of parents, schools and community in partnership that help a child to grow; it is certainly true that people *make* a society and a community.

The emotional health and well-being of individuals profoundly influences the way a society works and impacts on day-to-day behaviour. Examples would be a willingness or not to intervene when witnessing cruelty and/or bullying, attitude to neighbours and even, I would suggest, the type of entertainment that is preferred. Is it any accident, I wonder, that the highest selling video game is *Grand Theft Auto*, which is particularly violent, and that many comedy and reality television shows have a degree of humiliation at their core? In other words, the bidirectional influence that Bronfenbrenner (1979) hypothesized is a reality, with society impacting on individuals as well as individuals impacting on how a society's boundaries, rules and expectations shift and change. A very clear example is attitudes to smoking, which have changed over the last forty or so years, but attitudes to drinking have also changed though not in such a positive direction. There have always been people who drink too much, but the rise in liver problems in the young tells us that attitudes towards being drunk have altered. I am old enough to remember that a woman being drunk was seen as the worst kind of behaviour, while now it can be seen as a rite of passage on any social outing.

Another rather different example is how fashion can also influence the quality of relationships, such as the trend for forward facing buggies (i.e. facing away from the parent). The research carried out by Zeedyk (2008c) alluded to in Chapter 3 showed that babies and toddlers in forward facing buggies had far less interaction with their parents than those in more traditional prams and buggies that face towards the parent. While old-fashioned prams would certainly be very difficult to reintroduce, their height as well as their orientation meant that babies could not only face their parents but were almost at eye level. The style of a buggy seems such a simple thing, and yet its use has an impact on opportunities for parents and babies to interact with one another. As we saw from that chapter, such opportunities for interaction and communication are so important in the busy nature of day-to-day life.

Other aspects of modern daily life that seem to get in the way of communication include mobile phones, and people are often seen talking on their phone and not to the people they are with – whether other adults or babies. It is far too early – and probably in reality rather difficult – to assess how the pace of modern life and the related technology is influencing how children are developing, but just thinking about opportunities for real-life connection with another person may be diminishing, and how the brain seems to need such connection can give rise to concern.

Back to the child and behaviour

What this all means, of course, is that parents are bringing up their children, practitioners are working with children and families and teachers are teaching in a social atmosphere that affects every aspect of their daily life and work. The culture of celebrity has provided a great deal of anecdotal evidence from teacher colleagues who say that children's aspirations are to be on television or simply to be a 'celebrity'. The very phrases that imbue advertising such as 'must have', 'get it now', 'you're worth it' all help to promote a climate of expectations, which makes life for parents who are struggling financially, very difficult. Children are exposed to media influences far more than at any other time in our history and peer pressure, once children are in school, can become extremely powerful.

Children are also told that they 'have a voice', which of course is true, but this needs to be balanced by an understanding that children are just children and that sometimes adults need to take responsibility. Marano (2008), in his rather angry book entitled *A Nation of Wimps* which, while discussing current American society, nevertheless points to worrying trends in the way children are overprotected. Paradoxically, this does not seem to mean that they become stronger both physically and emotionally as adults but in fact are more likely to break down under any kind of stress. Elements of risk, even in this country, are constantly being eliminated with almost ludicrous rules of health and safety being established. This means that children begin to have no real sense of what is dangerous and what is safe, and also means that they can be more likely to take part in risky behaviour as teenagers (or younger) because of the lack of opportunities for safe risk taking.

If we recall Chapter 3, the baby's move away from the fixed attention to the mother after about three months to an interest in the surrounding world (while still very much needing the contact) indicates the first effort at independence and separation. Children do need to learn to 'stand on their own feet' but in a delicate balance between that safe base and safe haven. Even in the realm of education, the wish by some parents to encourage their children's development means that there is less importance placed on play and instead a stress on earlier and earlier introduction to formal reading and writing, which as we know disadvantages boys in particular, leading to difficulties in behaviour and emotional well-being. While there are many stalwart people in early years and education who fight constantly against this trend, there are still too many people who still seem to think that early is best. Without the capacity for play, for rough and tumble, to take some risks, children are not learning essential parts of their growing up.

The behaviour of children is a mirror to their inner self, but it also reflects the way they have been parented and in turn, as the circle of influence moves outward, this reflects not only parental history but also what society is saying to them about what is important. Their voices also carry on the wind of change which permeates every nook and cranny of every household, some of it so quietly that we hardly realize what is happening. To take a more general example, I wonder how many people have noticed the trend to use the word 'partner' rather than husband or wife, even amongst married couples?

What kind of society do we want?

The society we have is the society we deserve in many ways, and we bequeath a particular society to our children and in what we teach them about behaviour and attitudes towards one another. Many of the ceremonies that bound people together seem to be slowly disappearing. Many people do not attend church, which was as much a social as a religious event. Birthdays that marked a rite of passage such as twenty-one or eighteen also seem to be less prevalent. Engagements seem rare as people simply move in together, and in communities where parents work full time, there is often little opportunity for a gossip or to meet the neighbours. People, instead of talking and being with other people, can spend enormous amounts of time on the computer 'talking' to others on Facebook and similar social networking sites. These sites can be wonderful *tool* as a way of communication, but not as *the* method of communication. The human brain has developed over thousands of years to connect with other human beings, to notice facial expression, to respond to a touch – these are not possible on a computer.

The baby born today is surrounded by wonderful and amazing technology that will become part and parcel of his or her life, but the baby will also need people in order to grow in every aspect of their development. How this baby will behave, how they learn to understand others, to play, learn and ultimately work and live alongside and with a new family will rest on the relationships formed in those earliest years. The pace of learning cannot be rushed; the child will grow not only to the beat of their own drum but to the essential heartbeat of human life which will allow their development to unfold. What they will actually learn will depend on what we adults present as our gift, the society we have created, its attitudes and restrictions. The type of behaviour we get in a child is the type of behaviour that we have helped to engender from the very best to the very worst.

The child truly is father to the man – what sort of man or woman the child will be rests in our hands and our ability to understand the profound nature of being human and the simplicity of basic, fundamental needs.

Notes

I Introduction

1 I have used this phrase before in other texts as it is often so pertinent!
2 Dugatkin, incidentally, is a researcher who is also interested in play behaviours across species and has discovered that, like us, much learning also takes place during play. An interesting quote some years ago by Karl Groos (1976) in his study of primates states that they do not play because they are young, they have their youth in order to play, which gives us pause when thinking about what may be the repercussions for those children who have few opportunities for play.
3 David Sheldrick Wildlife Trust: www.sheldrickwildlifetrust.org.

2 A journey through the brain and the senses

1 See Robinson (2008) for an overview of these changes.
2 It is interesting to speculate whether the menopause in women and the 'midlife crisis' experienced by many men – often manifested in a desire for a Harley Davidson motorbike – is also associated with significant brain reorganization, which may be linked but also separate from changes related to a brain that is simply ageing.
3 There is a real difficulty in some of the neuroscience texts that areas of the brain can be given different names dependent on the particular biological tradition the authors may have followed.
4 Dr MacLean was senior research scientist at the National Institute of Mental Health (USA). For those who may wish to read the theory in its original description, it is in his work *The Triune Brain in Evolution* (1990, New York, Plenum Press), but availability may be severely limited, with corresponding cost.
5 Incidentally, this study shows us that we have learned little about ethical treatment of children over the past years, as can be seen from the Channel 4 television programme *Boys and Girls Alone* where a similar scenario was devised.
6 Other structures which are itemized as forming part of the limbic system include the cingulate gyrus, fornix and septum. Confusingly, different authors do occasionally add or subtract a structure, but those itemized in the main text are common to most.
7 If we link this information with its role in memory formation, it is possible to see how memory and knowing where we are at any one time, as well as how to get somewhere, are so closely intertwined – and how often a scent can evoke memories of place as well as people.
8 Also see Siegel (2007) for further reading and a detailed breakdown of the structures and related posited functions within the prefrontal cortex.
9 In this chapter, Schore cites his own extensive research but his seminal and perhaps best

known work is *Affect Regulation and the Origin of the Self* (1994, Mahwa, Earlbaum), which was a culmination of ten years' intensive research into brain function, development and emotion.

10 See page 272 in Begley (2007) for Meaney et al.'s work from 1989–2004, but rat responses to stress had already been noted in the 1950s.

11 See Robinson (2008, p.44) for an overview of research into early brain maturation, and also see Cozolino (2006, p.47) for an overview of research of structural changes in the brain during adolescence and adulthood.

12 Gregory (2004) notes that 'the total number of synapses in the cortex of one person is about 200,000 times the population of the earth' (p.123).

13 Glutamate is the most common neurotransmitter in the brain.

14 I am using 'she' for ease rather than s/he, but 'she' refers to babies and children of both genders. I may sometimes refer to 'he' too, and the same rule applies.

15 www.elizabethjarmanltd.co.uk.

16 In the left hemisphere, the two language centres tend to focus on the production and comprehension of speech, while the language centres in the right hemisphere tend to focus on the emotional quality of the voice.

17 Interestingly, muscle and fat formation in girls in adolescence is quite different to boys, which again may provide some rationale as to why their abilities in gross and fine movement appear to be more advanced earlier. Muscular development in girls is perhaps not an evolutionary priority after puberty, so perhaps the same 'foundations' are not needed.

3 Interactions, relationships and emotional responses

1 For an overview of musical development in the foetus and first year of life, see Cummings Persellin (2005) pp.20–21 in Flohr, J.W., (Ed.) *The Musical Lives of Young Children* (2005, New Jersey, Pearson Education).

2 Think of the pleasure most can experience when we hear a blackbird or robin sing, which is not music in its strictest sense but certainly musical. We can hear joy in their song even if the ornithologists tell us that they are really only saying 'keep off my territory' or 'don't come near my nest'.

3 It seems particularly poignant to consider that hearing is apparently the sense that is the last to go when close to death – something that has been supported by EEG recordings of brain activity. Incidentally, it is the brain stem that is fully developed at birth and is also the last bit of the brain to die.

4 Trevarthen (2008) notes that 'natural mother–infant protoconversations and baby songs have a period of around twenty to forty seconds.'

5 Beatrice Beebe, Ph.D., is a psychoanalyst and an infant researcher. She is a Clinical Professor of Medical Psychology and has worked extensively with parents and infants, especially in traumatic and/or abusive relationships. Particular work has been in analysing face-to-face interactions via video. She has taught and written extensively, and while based in the United States has visited Britain to deliver workshops on mother–infant interaction.

6 Babies with colic or who are more 'jittery' or 'fussy' can have longer and more sustained periods of intense crying, which can be very distressing for parents as comforting appears to be extremely difficult. Interestingly, a very small (and rather old) study by Larson and Allyon (1990) suggested that some infants were soothed when their quiet times were 'reinforced' by parental attention and music, which makes one wonder again at the role of the particular quality of motherese.

7 November 2009, www.nsf.gov.

8 Interestingly, this particular study did not find different levels of activation when these mothers looked at the distressed face of their own and an unknown baby. Perhaps evolution has a place here in that a crying baby needs comfort from whoever is around. Crying

represents danger, while smiling does not (usually!), and therefore a response can be more specific.

9 I suggest that this goes for teenagers and adults too – the lack of early nurture will influence their own emotional compass in their relationships.

10 The discovery was accidental, like so many other profound discoveries.

11 The classic studies were by Meltzoff and Moore (1983, 1989), involving forty newborn infants – the oldest being seventy-two hours old and the youngest just 42 minutes.

12 References to mother will also include a father's interactions and those of other adult carers.

13 See Paul Hart's chapter 'A walk in the Park' in Zeedyk (2008a)

14 Sadly, this idea seems to be re-emerging in some quarters where advice is given to mothers not to pick up their babies and let them cry. Somehow this seems worse in an age when we have all the years of research into attachment, the findings of brain imaging studies and general neuroscientific research all pointing to the necessity for comfort.

4 Time-related emergence of skills and abilities, growth and change

1 In addition, in Chisholm's study, one child (at age seven and adopted for three years) had been diagnosed with attention deficit hyperactivity disorder (ADHD) suggesting too that the lack of emotional stability in the early years had not only led to her needing a great deal of time to learn the 'safe person' but also her capacity to attend and focus.

2 We only have to consider how women who live together can find that their menstrual cycles begin to synchronize.

3 For loving parents, this must be such a pleasurable time as they can share and wonder at the baby's excitement at what, to adults, can seem quite mundane experiences, but to the baby something new can be a source of joy.

4 The seeking system is another of what Panksepp hypothesizes to be innate brain circuits and they include separation distress, play, care, fear, panic, rage and (in adults) lust, linking these systems to both animal and human behaviour.

5 I don't believe that these abilities emerging at similar times are coincidental but instead are highly interlinked and supportive of one another. However, while some links may be more obvious, others are potentially more difficult to assess. For example ascertaining whether a child's lack of mobility for whatever reason at this time influenced the development of their understanding of permanence.

6 See Robinson (2008) for an overview of research into facial processing.

7 See Crittenden and Clausen (2007) pp.353–357 for an explanation of her model.

8 Try to stop your hand shaping itself around your cup of coffee as you reach for it, or your pen or a spoon – it is virtually impossible because the patterns are so well established. It also explains why it is so difficult to adjust a way of holding a tennis racquet or changing a dance step once learned in a particular way. We also tend to have a pattern of how we dress and wash ourselves. Notice which side you wash first in the morning or what garment you always tend to put on first.

9 For a full description of the experiment, see pp.36–37 in Gopnik et al. (1999).

10 If any readers are familiar with the British television programme 'Father Ted', they may remember a sequence when on holiday in a caravan, Ted and Dougal play hide and seek. Dougal hides behind a curtain but his lower body and legs are showing – a wonderful and hilarious example of this lack of perspective.

11 A standard test for this is the 'Smartie experiment', where children aged between three and a half years and four and a half are shown a large tube of Smarties or similar. They are asked what they think is inside and they usually answer correctly, chocolates or sweets. They are then shown the contents, which could be pencils. Once the pencils are replaced, the lid put on, all within view of the child, they are then asked what someone else might

think is in the box. The younger age range usually reply 'pencils' because that is what they know. It is only the older children that reliably will say chocolates and so demonstrate that they are able to move away from their own understanding to take on another perspective. It is this ability that constitutes a 'theory of mind' in its most basic form.

12 This study followed these children from birth, followed up at age three and then every two years until they were aged thirty-two. In 2010, the study members will be returning for an assessment at age thirty-eight. The study has produced a plethora of findings that ultimately reinforce the necessity of early intervention if difficulties are emerging and that early troubles can also lead to a range of health difficulties in adulthood – also supported by the Felitti reports (1998/2003).

5 The adult: awareness, sensitivity, interpretation and responses

1 These are usually denial/protest, anger, bargaining, depression/extreme sadness and acceptance.

2 Hence the age-old question of nurses, 'Have your bowels moved today?' I will always remember from my nursing days a patient saying to me, 'No, they're where they have always been!' – an old joke I know, but it did make me smile.

3 See, for example, Kahn's (2006) summary report on involving fathers in preschool settings commissioned by the DfES available at www.pre-school.org.uk/research/pdf/Involvingfathers; also www.fatherhoodinstitute.org and www.literacytrust.org.

4 The Fibonacci series is formed by adding two numbers to yield a third number and repeating the process to form a sequence, e.g. $1 + 1 = 2, 1 + 2 = 3, 2 + 3 = 5$ and so on.

5 This document, which is all about 'creating enabling environments for children', also comes with a DVD. The Oxfordshire County Council Sure Start programme can be contacted for further details.

6 The authors of this programme are: Glen Cooper, Kent Hoffman and Bert Powell from Marycliff Institute in Spokane, WA; and Robert Marvin from the University of Virginia in Charlottesville, VA. Details of the project and their work can be found at www.circleofsecurity.org.

6 Behaviour as the self's mirror

1 These measure glucose uptake in the brain and other soft tissue areas.

2 These use strong magnets and pulses of radio waves to obtain detailed images.

3 Bronfenbrenner was the co-founder of Head Start in the United States. An introduction to his bio-ecological systems theory can be found at: http://pt3.nl.edu/paquetteryanwebquest.pdf.

4 Mary was convicted of the manslaughter of two young boys but her horrendous background of abuse was taken into account. Her mother apparently did sell her stories to newspapers and later Mary also appeared to give some of her story.

5 www.centreforsocialjustice.org.uk.

6 'Giving children the best start in life' *Policy and Developments from Birth to the End of the Foundation Stage* (2006, Crown Copyright). This policy is built around the Children's Bill and Every Child Matters, encapsulating the former British Labour Government's ten-year plan for Children's services.

Bibliography

Allman, J., (2000) *Evolving Brains*: New York, Scientific American Library

Atkinson, J., (2000) *The Developing Visual Brain*: Oxford, Oxford University Press

Bear, M.F., Connors, B.W., Paradiso, M.A., (1996) *Neuroscience, Exploring the Brain*: Baltimore, Williams & Wilkins

Begley, S., (2007) *Train Your Mind, Change Your Brain*: New York, Ballantine Books

Ben-Sasson, A., Cermak, S.A., Orsmond, G.I., Carter, A.S., Fogg, L., (2007) Can we differentiate sensory over-responsivity from anxiety symptoms in toddlers? *Perspectives of Occupational Therapists and Psychologists in Infant Mental Health Journal*, 28, Sep–Oct., 536–558

Benes, F.M., Turtle, M., Khan, Y., Farol, P., (1994) Myelination of a key relay zone in the hippocampal formation occurs in the human brain during childhood, adolescence and adulthood: *Archives of General Psychiatry*, 51, June

Berry Brazelton, T., Sparrow, J.D., (2006) *Touchpoints Birth to Three*: Cambridge, MA, Merloyd Lawrence

Bergman, K., Sarka, P., O'Connor, T.J., Modi, N., Glover, V., (2007) Maternal stress during pregnancy predicts cognitive ability and fearfulness in infancy: *Journal Am. Acad. Child Adolesc. Psychiatry*, 46 (11)

Berthoz, A., (2000) *The Brain's Sense of Movement*: London, Harvard University Press

Biddulph, S., (2006) *Raising Babies*: London, Harper Collins

Bowlby, J., (1951) *Maternal Care and Mental Health* (WHO Monograph, No.2): Geneva, World Health Organisation

Bowlby, J., (1953) *Child Care and the Growth of Love*: London, Pelican Books

Bowlby, J., (1969/1991) *Attachment and Loss, Vol. 1, Attachment*: London, Penguin

Bowlby, J., (1973/1991) *Attachment and Loss, Vol. 2, Separation*: London, Penguin

Bowlby J., (1980/1991) *Attachment and Loss Vol. 3, Loss*: London, Penguin

Bowlby J., (1988) *A Secure Base*: London, Routledge

Braun, A. K., Bock, J., (2007) Born to learn: early learning optimises brain function: in Gruhn, W. and Rauscher, F. (Eds), *Neurosciences in Music Pedagogy*, pp.27–51

Breakdown Britain, (2006) Social Justice Policy Group: London, Centre for Social Justice

Breakthrough Britain, (2007) Social Justice Policy Group: London, Centre for Social Justice

British Medical Association Board of Science, (2006) *Child and Adolescent Mental Health – A guide for health care professionals*: London, BMA

Bronfenbrenner, U., (1979) *The Ecology of Human Development*: Cambridge, MA, Harvard University Press

Budiansky, S., (2003) *The Truth About Dogs*: London, Penguin

Cacioppo, J.T., Patrick, W., (2008) *Loneliness*: New York, Norton

Caldwell, P., Horwood, J., (2008) *Using Intensive Interaction and Sensory Integration*: London, Jessica Kingsley

Carter R., (2000) *Mapping the Mind*: London, Phoenix

Cavanagh, P., (2005) The artist as neuroscientist, *Nature*, 434, 301–307

Chisholm, K., (2007) Attachment in children adopted from Romanian orphanages: in Crittenden, P.M. and Claussen, A.H. (Eds), *The Organization of Attachment Relationships, Maturation, Culture and Context*: New York, Cambridge University Press

Christensson, K., Cabrera, T., Christensson, E., Uvnas-Moberg, K., Winberg, J., (1994) Separation distress call in the human neonate in the absence of maternal body contact: *Acta Paediatrica*, 84 (5), 468–473. Published online 21 January 2008

Cozolino, L., (2006) *The Neuroscience of Human Relationships*: New York, Norton

Crittenden, P.M., (1999) Danger and development: the organisation of self-protective strategies: *Monographs Society Research Child Development*, 64 (3)

Crittenden, P.M., Claussen, A.H. (Eds), (2000) *The Organisation of Attachment Relationships*: Cambridge, Cambridge University Press

Crittenden, P.M., (2002) *Attachment, Information Processing and Psychiatric Disorder: Special Article*: Miami, FL, Family Relations Institute

Crittenden, P.M., (2005) Attachment theory, psychopathology and psychotherapy: the dynamic-maturational approach: *Psicoterapia*, 30, 171–182

Crittenden, P.M., (2008) *Raising Parents: Attachment, parenting and child safety*: Cullompton, Willan Publishers

Crittenden, P.M., Clausen, A.H., (Eds), (2007) *The Organization of Attachment Relationships, Maturation, Culture and Context*: New York, Cambridge University Press

Crittenden, P.M., Lang, C., Clausen, A.H., Partridge, M., (2007) Relations among mother's dispositional representations of parenting: in Crittenden, P.M. et al. (Eds), *The Organization of Attachment Relationships, Maturation, Culture and Context*: New York, Cambridge University Press

Cummings Persellin, D., (2005) Foundations, music learning and development: in Flohr, J.W. (Ed.), *The Musical Lives of Young Children*: New Jersey, Pearson Education

Cunningham, H., (2006) *The Invention of Childhood*: London, BBC Books

Cupchik, C., Philips, K., Truong, H., (2005) Sensitivity to the cognitive and affective qualities of odours: *Cognition and Emotion*, 19 (1), 121–131

Damasio, A., (1999) *The Feeling of What Happens*: New York, Harcourt Brace

DCSF, (2007) *The Children's Plan: Building brighter futures*: London, DCSF

DCSF, (2009) *The Protection of Children in England: A progress report, the Lord Laming Review*: London, DCS

DCSF, (2007) *The Children's Plan: Building brighter futures*: London, DCSF

DCSF, (2009) *Healthy Lives, Brighter Futures*: London, DCSF

Derrington, A., (2002) From retina to cortex: in Roberts, D., (Ed), *Signals and Perception*: Oxford, Open University Press, 147–60

DfES, (2004) *Every Child Matters: Change for children*: London, DfES

Dube, S.R., Felitti, V.J., Dong, M., Giles, W.H., Anda, R.F., (2003) The impact of adverse childhood experiences on health problems: evidence from four birth cohorts dating back to 1900: *Preventative Medicine*, 37 (3), 268–277

Dugatkin, L.E., (2002a) Watching culture shape even guppy love: *Cerebrum*, 4 (1), Winter, 51–66

Dugatkin, L.E., (2002b) Prancing primates, turtles with toys: *Cerebrum*, 4(3), Summer, 41–52

Duncan Smith, I., Allen, G., (2008) *Early Intervention, Good Parents, Great Kids, Better Citizens*: London, Centre for Social Justice/The Smith Institute

Edwards, R.D., Hodges, D.A., (2007) Neuromusical research: an overview of the literature: in Gruhn & Rauscher (Eds), *Neurosciences and Music Pedagogy*: New York, Nova Science Publishers

Ekman, P., (2004) *Emotions Revealed – understanding faces and feelings*: London, Orion

Ekman, P., Davidson, R.J. (Eds), (1994) *The Nature of Emotion*: Oxford, Oxford University Press

Elfer P., Goldschmied, E., Selleck, D., (2003) *Key Persons in the Nursery*: London, David Fulton

Felitti, V.J., Anda, R.F., Nordenberg, D., Williamson, D.F., Spitz, A.M., Edwards, V., Koss, M.P., Marks, J.S., (1998) Relationship of childhood abuse and household dysfunction to many of the leading causes of death in adults. The adverse childhood experiences (ACE) study: *American Journal of Preventative Medicine*, 14, 245–258

Feinberg, T.E., Keenan, J.P., (2005) *The Lost Self*: Oxford, Oxford University Press

Field, T., Diego, M., Dieter, J., Hernandez-Reif, M., Schanberg, S., Kuhn, C., Yando, R., Bendell, D., (2004) Prenatal depression effects on the fetus and the newborn: *Infant Behavior and Development*, 27, 216–229

Filippi, C.G., Ulug, A.M., Deck, M.D., Zimmerman, R.D., Heier, L.A., (2002) Developmental delay in children: assessment with proton MR spectroscopy: *American Journal of Neuroradiology*, 23 (5), 882–888

Fischer, K., (2005) *Dynamics of Cognitive and Brain Development and Education*: Paper presented at launch meeting in Cambridge UK for Centre for Neuroscience in Education, July

Flohr, J.W. (Ed.), (2005) *The Musical Lives of Young Children*: Upper Saddle River, NJ, Pearson Education

Flohr, J.W., Trevarthen, C., (2007) Music learning in childhood, early developments of a musical brain and body: in Gruhn, W. and Rauscher, F. (Eds), *Neurosciences in Music Pedagogy*, pp.53–99

Fox, N., Calkin, S.D., Bell, M.A., (1994) *Neural Plasticity and Development in the First Two Years of Life: Evidence from cognitive and socioemotional domains of research*: New York, Cambridge University Press

Fox, N., Davidson, R.J., (1984) *The Psychobiology of Affective Development*: Hillsdale, NJ, Lawrence Erlbaum

Fries, A., (2005) Early experience in humans is associated with changes in neuropeptides critical for regulating social behaviour: *Proceedings of the National Academy of Sciences of the USA*, 102 (47), 17237–17240

Gallese, V., (2001) The 'shared manifold' hypothesis –from mirror neurons to empathy: *Journal of Consciousness Studies*, 8 (5–7), 33–50

Gattis, M., Bekkering, H., Wohlschlager, A., (2002) Goal directed imitation: in Meltzoff, A.N. and Prinz, W. (Eds), *The Imitative Mind*: Cambridge, Cambridge University Press

Gazzaniga, M., (2008) *Human – the science behind what makes us unique*: New York, Harper Collins

Geddes, H., (2006) *Attachment in the Classroom*: London, Worth

Gerhardt, S., (2004) *Why Love Matters: How affection shapes a baby's brain*: London, Routledge

Goddard, S., (2005) *Reflexes, Learning and Behaviour* (2nd edition): Eugene, OR, Fern Ridge Press

Goldberg, E., (2001) *The Executive Brain*: Oxford, Oxford University Press

Goldschmied, E., Jackson, S., (1999) *People Under Three*: New York, Routledge

Goodlin, R.C., Schmidt, W., (1972) Human fetal arousal levels as indicated by heart rate recordings: *Am. J. Obstet. Gynecol.*, 114, 613–621

Gopnik, A., Meltzoff, A., Kuhl, P., (1999) *How Babies Think*: London, Weidenfield & Nicholson

Green, H., McGinity, A., Meltzer, H., Ford, T., Goodman, R., (2004) *Mental Health of Children and Young People in Great Britain*: London, Office of National Statistics, Palgrave MacMillan

Gregory, R.L. (Ed.), (2004) *The Oxford Companion to the Mind* (2nd edition); Oxford University Press

Grille, R., (2008) *Parenting for a Peaceful World*: Richmond, The Children's Project

Gross, K., (1976) *Plays of Animals*: Salem, NH, Ayer

Gruhn, W., Rauscher, F., (2007) *Neurosciences in Music Pedagogy*: New York, Nova Biomedical Books

Gunnar, M.R., (1998) Quality of early care and buffering of neuroendcorine stress reactions; Potential effects on the developing human brain: *Preventive Medecine*, 27, 208–211

Gur, R.C., (2005) Brain maturation and its relevance to understanding criminal culpability of juveniles: *Curr Psychiatry Rep.*, 7 (4), 292–296, Review

Hall, D., Hall, S., (2007) The 'Family–Nurse Partnership': developing an instrument for identification, assessment and recruitment of clients: *Research Report*, DCSF-RWO22: London, DCSF

Hodson, D., (Chair) (2009) *Every Family Matters*: A Policy report by the Family Law Review; London, Centre for Social Justice

Hosking, G., Walsh, I., (2005) *Violence and What to Do About It: The WAVE Report*; Croydon, WAVE

Honing, H., Ladinig, O., Haden, G.P., Winkler, I., (2009) Is beat induction innate or learned? The neurosciences and music III – disorders and plasticity: *Annals of the New York Academy of Sciences*, 1169: 93–96

House of Commons, Health Committee, (2003) *The Victoria Climbie Inquiry Report and Formal Minutes*: London, The Stationary Office

Hughes, B., (2001) *Evolutionary Playwork and Reflective Analytic Practice*: London, Routledge

Iacoboni, M., (2008) *Mirroring People*: New York, Farrar, Strauss & Giroux

Jackson, S., (2009) Close to you: *Nursery World*, 30 April

Jaffe, J., Beebe, B., Felstein, S., Crown, C., (2001) Rhythms of dialogue in infancy: coordinated timing and social development: *Society of Child development Monographs*, Serial No. 265, 66 (2)

Johnson, M.H., (2001) Functional brain development in humans: *Nature Reviews: Neuroscience*, 2, July, 474–483

Johnston, M.V., (1995) Neurotransmitters and vulnerability of the developing brain: *Brain & Development*, 17: 301–306

Kahn, T., (2006) *Fathers' Involvement in Early Years Settings: Findings from Research*: London, Department for Education and Skills. Available at www.pre-school.org.uk/research/pdf/ Involvingfathers.

Karr-Morse, R., Wiley, M.S., (1997) *Ghosts from the Nursery: Tracing the roots of violence*: New York, Atlantic Monthly Press

Knickmeyer, R., Gouttard, S., Kang, C., Evans, D., Wilber, K., Smith, K., Hamer, R.M., Lin, W., Gilmore, J.H., (2008) A structural MRI study of human brain development from birth to 2 years: *Journal of Neuroscience*, November, 19, 12176–12182

Kugiumutzakis, G., (1998) Neonatal imitation in the intersubjective companion space: in Braten, S. (Ed.), *Intersubjective Communication and Emotion in Early Ontogeny*: Cambridge, Cambridge University Press.

Kugiumutzakis, G., Kokkinaki, T., Makrodimitaki, M., Vitalaki, E., (2005) Emotions in early mimesis: in Nadel, J., Muir, D. (eds), *Emotional Development*: Oxford, Oxford University Press

Laming, Lord (Chair), (2003) *The Victoria Climbié Inquiry*: Norwich, HMSO. Downloadable PDF file available at www.publicationseverychildmatters.gov.uk

Larson K., Allyon, T., (1990) The effects of contingent music and differential reinforcement on infantile colic: *Journal of Behaviour Research and Therapy*, 28 (2), 119–125

Layard, R., Dunn, J., (2009) *A Good Childhood*: London, The Children's Society

LeDoux, J., (1998) *The Emotional Brain*: London, Weidenfield & Nicholson

Leslie, A., (1987) Pretence and representation, the origins of 'theory of mind': *Psychological Review*, 94 (4), 412–446

Levin, F.M., (2009) *Emotion and the Psychodynamics of the Cerebellum*: London, Karnac

Levitin, D.J., (2006) *This is Your Brain on Music*: London, Penguin

Lewis, T.L., Amini, F., Lannon, R., (2000) *A General Theory of Love*: New York, Vintage

Lieberman, A.E., Compton, N.C., Van Horn, P., Ippen, C.G., (2003) *Losing a Parent to Death in the Early Years*: Washington, D.C., Zero to Three Press

Lillard, A., (2002) Pretend Play and Cognitive Development, in Goswami, U. (Ed.), *Childhood Cognitive Development*: Oxford, Blackwell

Llinas, R.R., (2002) *I of the Vortex; From neurons to the self*: Cambridge, MA, MIT Press

Locke, J.L., (1995), *The Child's Path to Spoken Language* (2nd edition): London, Harvard University Press

Lorch, C.A., Lorch, V., Deifendor, A.O., Early, P.W., (1994) Effect of stimulative and sedative music on systolic blood pressure, heart rate, and respiratory rate in premature infants: *Journal of Music Therapy*, 31, 105–118

MacLean, P.D., (1990) *The Triune Brain in Evolution: Role in paleocerebral functions*: New York, Plenum

Marano, H.E., (2008) *A Nation of Wimps*: New York, Broadway Books

Matsuzawa, J., Matsui, M., Konishi, T., Noguchi, K., Gur, R.C., Bilker, W., Miyawaki, T., (2001) Age-related volumetric changes of brain gray and white matter in healthy infants and children: *Cerebral Cortex*, 11 (4), 335–342

McClure, A., (2008) *Making it Better for Boys in Schools, Families and Communities*: London, Continuum

McElwain, N.L., (2006) Maternal sensitivity to infant distress and nondistress as predictors of infant-mother attachment security: *Journal of Family Psychology*, 2 (2), 247–255

Meaney, M.J., Francis, D.D., Diorio, J., Liu,D., (1999) Nongenomic transmission across generations in maternal behaviour and stress responses in the rat: *Science*, 286, 1155–1158

Meltzoff, A.N., (1985) Immediate and deferred imitation in fourteen- and twenty-four month old Infants: *Child Development*, 56, 62–72

Meltzoff, A.N., (1999) Origins of theory of mind, cognition, and communication: *Journal of Communication Disorders*, 32, 251–269

Meltzoff, N.A., (2002a) Elements of a developmental theory of imitation: in Meltzoff and Prinz (Eds), *The Imitative Mind*: Cambridge, Cambridge University Press

Meltzoff, A.N., (2002b) Imitation as a mechanism of social cognition: origins of empathy, theory of mind and the representation of action: in Smith, P.K. and Hart, C.H. (Eds), *Handbook of Psychological Development*: Oxford, Blackwell

Meltzoff, A.N., Moore, M.K., (1983) Newborn infants imitate adult facial gestures: *Child Development*, 54, 702–709

Meltzoff, N.A., Moore, M.K., (1989) Imitation in newborn infants: exploring the range of gestures imitated and the underlying mechanisms: *Developmental Psychology*, 25, 954–962

Meltzoff, A.N., Prinz, W., (2002a) *The Imitative Mind*: Cambridge, Cambridge University Press

Meltzoff, A.N., Prinz, W., (2002b) An introduction to the imitative mind and brain: in Meltzoff and Prinz (Eds), *The Imitative Mind*: Cambridge, Cambridge University Press

Messinger, D.S., (2002) Positive and negative: infant facial expressions and emotions: *Current Directions in Psychological Science*: 11 (1), 1–6

Music, G., (2005) Surfacing the depths: thoughts on imitation, resonance and growth: *Journal of Child Psychotherapy*, 31 (1), 72–90

Nagy, E., (2008) Innate intersubjectivity: newborns' sensitivity to communication disturbance; *Developmental Psychology*, 44 (6), 1779–1784

Newberger, E.H., (1999) *The Men They Will Become*: Reading, MA, Perseus

Nelson, C.A., Bosquet, M., (2005) Neurobiology of fetal and infant development: implications for infant mental health: in Zeanah, C.H. Jr. (Ed.), *Handbook of Infant Mental Health*: New York, The Guilford Press

O'Connor, T.G., Heron, J., Golding, J., Beveridge, M., Glover, V., (2002) Maternal antenatal anxiety and children's behavioural/emotional problems at 4 years: *The British Journal of Psychiatry*, 180: 502–508

O'Neill, M., Jones, M.C., Zeedyk, M.S., (2008) The use of imitation with children with autistic spectrum disorder: foundations for shared communication: in Zeedyk, M.S., (Ed.), *Promoting Interaction for Individuals with Communicative Impairments*: London, Jessica Kinglsey

Palmer, S., (2006) *Toxic Childhood*: London, Orion

Panksepp, J., (1998) *Affective Neuroscience*: New York, Oxford University Press

Paus, T., Zijdenbos, A., Worsley, K., Collins, D.L., Blumenthal, J., Giedd, J.N., Rapoport, J.L., Evans, A.C., (1999) Structural maturation of neural pathways in children and adolescents: in vivo study: *Science*, 283, 1908–1911

Perry, B., (2006) Applying principles of neurodevelopment to clinical work with maltreated and traumatised children: in Boyd Webb, N. (Ed.), *Working with Traumatised Youth in Child Welfare*: New York, Guilford Press

Piaget, J., (1959/2002) *The Language and Thought of the Child*: London, Routledge Classics

Prior, V., Glaser, D., (2007) *Understanding Attachment and Attachment Disorders*: London, Jessica Kingsley

Quartz, S., Sejnowski, T.J., (2002) *Liars, Lovers and Heroes*: New York, Harper Collins

Ramachandran, V.S., Oberman, L.M., (2006) Broken mirrors: a theory of autism: *Scientific American*, 16 October

Read, V., (2010) *Developing Attachment in Early Years Settings*: Abingdon, Routledge

Reddy, V., (2008) *How Infants Know Minds*: London, Harvard University Press

Rizolatti, G., Camarda, R., Gallese, V., Fogassi, L., (1995) Premotor cortex and the recognition of motor actions: *Cognitive Brain Research* 3, 131–141

Rizzolatti, G., Fadiga, L., Fogassi, L., Gallese, V., (2002) From mirror neurons to imitation: facts and speculation: in Meltzoff and Prinz (Eds), *The Imitative Mind*, pp. 247–266

Robinson, M., (1997) *Pretend Play*, A study of the content and characteristics of pretend play in a group of pre-school children at a family centre: Unpublished masters' dissertation, Tavistock and Portman NHS Trust

Robinson, M., (2003) *From Birth to One*: Maidenhead, Open University Press

Robinson, M., (2008) *Development from Birth to Eight*: Maidenhead, Open University Press

Sachs, O., (2007) *Musicophilia*: New York, Random House

Sallenbach, W.B., (1993) The intelligent prenate: paradigms in prenatal learning and bonding: in Thomas Blum (Ed.), *Prenatal Perception, Learning and Bonding*: Berlin, Leonardo, p.73

Sax, L., (2006) *Why Gender Matters*: New York, Broadway Books

Sax, L., (2007) *Boys Adrift*: New York, Basic Books

Sheets-Johnstone, M., (1999) *The Primacy of Movement*; Amsterdam/Philadelphia, PA, John Benjamins

Schiffman, H.R., (2001) *Sensation and Perception* (5th edition): New York, Wiley

Schofield, G., Beek, M., (2007) *Attachment Handbook for Foster Care and Adoption*: London, BAAF

Schonkoff, J.P., Philips, D.A. (Eds), (2000) *From Neurons to Neighbourhoods: The Science of Early Childhood Development*: Washington, D.C., National Academy Press

Schore, A., (1994) *Affect Regulation and the Origin of the Self*: Mahwah, NJ, Erlbaum

Schore, A., (2003) Early relational trauma, disorganised attachment and the development of a predisposition to violence: in Solomon, M.F., Siegel, D.J. (Eds), *Healing Trauma, Attachment, Mind, Body and Brain*: New York, Norton

Siegel, D.J., (2003) An interpersonal neurobiology of psychotherapy: the developing mind and the resolution of trauma: in Solomon, M.F., Siegel, D.J. (Eds), *Healing Trauma, Attachment, Mind, Body And Brain*: New York, Norton

Siegel, D.J., (2007) *The Mindful Brain*: New York, Norton

Solomon, M.F., Siegel, D.J. (Eds), (2003) *Healing Trauma, Attachment, Mind, Body and Brain*: New York, Norton

St. Clair, C., Danon-Boileau, L., Trevarthen, C., (2007) Signs of autism in infancy: sensitivity for the rhythms of expression in communication: in Acquarone, S. (Ed.), *Signs of Autism in Infancy*, London, Karnac Books

Stokes, G., (2009) *And the Music Still Plays: Stories of people with dementia*: London, Hawker

Stoodley, C.J., Stein, J.F., (2009) The cerebellum and dyslexia: *Cortex*, October

Strathearn, L., Li, J., Fonagy, P., Read Mantague, P., (2008) What's in a smile? Maternal responses to infant facial cues: *Paediatrics*, 122, 40–51

Soussignan, R., Schaal, B., (2005) Emotional processes in human newborns: a functionalist perspective: in Nadel, J., Muir, D. (Eds), *Emotional Development*: Oxford, Oxford University Press

Sunderland, M., (2006) *The Science of Parenting*: London, Dorland Kindersley

Talge, N., Neal, C., Glover, V., and the Early Stress, Translational Research and Prevention Science Network: Fetal and Neonatal Experience on Child and Adolescent Mental Health, (2007): Antenatal maternal stress and long-term effects on child neurodevelopment: how and why? *Journal of Child Psychology and Psychiatry*, 48, (3/4), 245–261

Trevarthen, C., (2004) Brain development, in Gregory, R.L. (Ed.), *Oxford Companion to the Mind* (2nd edition); Oxford, New York, Oxford University Press, pp.116–127

Trevarthen, C., (2005) First things first: infants make good use of the sympathetic rhythm of imitation, without reason or language: *Journal of Child Psychotherapy*, 31 (1), 91–113

Trevarthen, C., (2006) *Harmony in Meaning: How infants use their innate musicality to find companions in culture*. Paper presented at the Symposium on 'Music and Universal Harmony' in Honour of Mikis Theodorakis, University of Crete, 10–11 March

Trevarthen, C., (2007a) The musical art of infant conversation: narrating in the time of sympathetic experience, without rational interpretation, before words: Paper submitted for publication in *Musicae Scientiae*

Trevarthen, C., (2007b) *Rhythm and Sympathy*: Paper presented at the Touch Learn Conference, 8–10 May, Coventry, UK.

Trevarthen, C., (2008) Intuition for human communication: in Zeedyk, M.S. (Ed.), *Promoting Social Interaction for Individuals with Communicative Impairments*: London, Jessica Kingsley

Tronick, E., (2007) The Neurobehavioural and Social-Emotional Development of Infants and Children: New York, Norton

Tronick, E., Als, H., Adamson, L., Wise, S., Berry Brazelton, T., (1978) The infant's response to entrapment between contradictory messages in face to face interaction: *Journal of the American Academy of Psychiatry*, 17, 1–13

Valentin, D., Herve, A., (2003) Early face recognition: what can we learn from a myopic baby neural network?: in Pascalis, O., and Slater, A. (Eds), *The Development of Face Processing in Infancy and Early Childhood*: New York, Nova Science Publishers

Williams, J.H.G., Whiten, A., Suddendorf, T., Perrett, D.I., (2001) Imitation, mirror neurons and autism: *Neuroscience and Biobehavioural Reviews*, 25, 287–295

Wolf, M., (2008) *Proust and the Squid: The story and science of the reading brain*: Cambridge, Icon Books

Zeanah, C.H. Jr. (Ed.), (2005) *Handbook of Infant Mental Health*: New York, Guilford Press

Zeedyk, S., (2008a) *Promoting Social Interaction for Individuals with Communicative Impairments*: London, Jessica Kingsley

Zeedyk, S., (2008b) *Children at Peace with Themselves*: Inaugural Goodman Lecture, Cambridge, May. Available for download at www.whataboutthechildren.org.uk.

Zeedyk, S., (2008c) What's life in a baby buggy like?: The impact of buggy orientation on parent–infant interaction and infant stress: Study conducted in collaboration with National Literacy Trust (www.literacytrust.org.uk)

Index

ADHD (attention deficit hyperactivity
   disorder) 109n1
adopted children 86
adrenal gland 13
adults: awareness and sensitivity 2, 78–97;
   emotional needs 38–9, 78–80; emotional
   regulation 81–2; environment 94–7; fears
   and phobias 87–9; gender differences 91–
   4; interpreting behaviour 89–91;
   key person approach 82–4, 95; loss
   and grief 85–7; responsibility 80–1;
   separations and settling 84–5; working
   with parents 91; *see also* interactions and
   relationships; mothers
Adverse Child Experiences Report
   (ACE) 101–2
aggression 5, 65, 76, 77, 93
Ainsworth, M. 55
alcohol 62–3, 104
Allyon, T. 108n6
amygdala 12–13, 17, 65
anger 81, 93
animals: attachment 45, 54; children's
   reactions to 88; communication 3–4;
   imitation 51, 52; play 75
anxiety: antenatal 40; in attachment 55,
   65–6, 79; in children 83, 84; stranger
   anxiety 64–5, 68
association areas 9, 19
at-risk children 76, 80
Atkinson, J. 29
attachment: and brain development 17, 53;
   as defence 13, 54–5; and identity 59;
   needs 44, 82–4; security 64–6, 75; and
   sharing 12; *see also* Circle of Security
attention 62
attention deficit hyperactivity disorder
   (ADHD) 109n1

attention-getting 71–2
autism 20, 50, 51, 52–3, 85
autonomic nervous system 12
avoidant children 55, 65–6, 84–5
axons 21

Baby Peter 80
balance 32–3
Bear, M.F. et al. 13, 19
Beebe, B. 44
Beek, M. 54
Begley, S. 18
behaviour: action and inhibition 35;
   age-related changes 56–7; conduct
   disorders 49; criminal responsibility 100;
   and emotions 2, 6; expectations and
   boundaries 4–6, 55, 57, 74, 77, 96,
   104; and gender 5, 49, 57–8; influences
   on 98–105; interpreting behaviour 89–91
behaviour management 3, 54, 100–1
behaviourism 54
Bell, Mary 100
Ben-Sasson, A. et al. 90
Bergman, K. et al. 40
Berry Brazelton, T. 48, 60, 68
Berthoz, A. 35, 36
Biddulph, S. 102
bio-ecological systems theory 99, 104
Bock, J. 42–3, 44
bodily awareness 68, 69, 87–8
Bosquet, M. 23–4
boundaries: behaviour 4–6, 55, 57, 74, 96,
   104; body 68
Bowlby, J. 54
brain development 9–11, 16, 17, 18–24;
   and communication 39, 93; gender
   differences 5, 93
brain imaging 98

brain stem 11–12, 47
brain structure and function 8–24, 98;
    association areas 9, 19; asymmetry 16;
    brain stem 11–12, 47; cerebellum 19–20,
    41; corpus callosum 17–18, 28; cortex
    (cerebrum) 14–18; dominance 24;
    hemispheres 9, 14, 16–17, 24, 31, 32, 35,
    42; myelination 22, 23; neurons 20–2;
    plasticity 23–4; subcortical (emotional)
    brain 12–14; synapses 21, 22–3
Braun, A.K. 42–3, 44
breastfeeding 61
'broccoli experiment' 68–9
Bronfenbrenner, U. 99, 103
Budiansky, S. 32
buggies 44, 104
Bulger, Jamie 100
bullying 72, 81, 104

Cacioppo, J.T. 46, 51, 52, 101
Caldwell, P. 27, 52
Carter, R. 25
Cavanagh, P. 44
Centre for Social Justice 101
cerebellum 19–20, 41
cerebrum 14–18
child development 6, 56–77; early
    weeks 58–9; first year 59–67; influences
    on 99–105; second year 67–70, 75;
    see also fears and phobias; play; temper
    tantrums
childhood 99–105
Children's Act (2004) 103
Children's Commissioner 103
Children's Trusts 103
Chisholm, K. 59, 64, 109n1
choice and control 66, 67, 84
Christensson, K. et al. 45
Circle of Security 95
Clausen, A.H. 55, 91
Climbié, Victoria 80, 103
clumsiness 36
colour 29, 31, 34, 94
communication 3–4; and brain
    development 39, 93; gender
    differences 93; and hearing 31–3;
    imitation as communication 69; lack
    of 42–4, 60, 62, 104, 106; by touch 27;
    in the womb 39–40
concentration 62
conduct disorders 49
cooperation 75
corpus callosum 17–18, 28

cortex (cerebrum) 14–18
cortisol 13
Cozolino, L. 12, 13, 17, 47
criminal responsibility 100
Crittenden, P.M. et al. 13, 55, 57, 60, 65–7,
    84, 90–1
crying 45–6, 58
culture 4
Cunningham, H. 100
Cupchik, C. et al. 33–4
curiosity 62

Damasio, A. 13
dangers 64, 87–9, 105
dark, fear of the 88
David Sheldrick Wildlife Trust 4
Davidson, R.J. 18
day care 103
death 85
declarative memory 66
declarative pointing 63
dementia 3, 42, 98–9
dendrites 21
Department for Children, Schools and
    Families 103
dependence 68
depressed mothers 39, 43, 48
Derrington, A. 30
developmental delay 21
disappointment 71, 72
distress 13, 48, 64, 70, 71
divorce and separation 85–6, 101
dressing up 76
Dugatkin, L.E. 4
Dunedin longitudinal study 76, 110n12
Dunn, J. 101, 103
dynamic model of maturation (DMM) 65–6
dyslexia 20

eating 33
Edwards, R.D. 40, 42
Ekman, P. 47
Elfer, P. et al. 82, 83
emotional brain 12–14, 17, 47, 49, 64, 71
emotional disorders 48–9
emotional health and well-being 33–4,
    59–60, 101–4; see also attachment;
    separation anxiety
emotional regulation 15, 71, 77, 81–2
emotional responses 10, 17–18, 44, 45–6,
    49–50, 51, 52–3; see also attachment
emotions 1–2, 12, 24; adults'
    needs 38–9, 78–80; aggression 5,

65, 76, 77, 93; anger 81, 93; and
behaviour 2, 6; depression 39, 43, 48;
disappointment 71, 72; frustration 70,
71, 72–3; gender differences 48–9,
93–4; joyfulness 81; loneliness 58, 65–6;
storms of feeling 70, 71; *see also* anxiety;
distress; fears and phobias; self-awareness;
temper tantrums
empathy 69, 71, 75, 81–2
environment 94–7; caring 95–6;
indoor environment 96; outdoor
environment 96–7; stimuli 22
episodic memory 67
Every Child Matters 103
Every Family Matters 101
exercise 36
experience 9, 46
explicit memory 66, 67
exploration 28, 61–3
eye contact 29, 47–8, 49–50, 68

faces 29, 44, 46–50, 64
facial expressions 47, 48, 49–50, 52
Family–Nurse Partnership (FNP) 103
fantasy play 69, 74, 75, 76, 77
fears and phobias 12, 76, 81, 87–9
feeding 28
Felitti, V.J. et al. 102
Field, T. et al. 39
Filippi, C.G. et al. 21
Flohr, J.W. 40, 41, 42
focus 62
forebrain 10, 11
fostered children 86
Fox, N. 18
frontal lobe 14
frustration 70, 71, 72–3

Gattis, M. et al. 15–16
gaze 29, 47–8, 49–50
Geddes, H. 83
gender differences 91–4; awareness
of gender 69; behaviour 5, 49,
57–8; brain development 5, 93; colour
perception 31, 94; communication 93;
emotions 48–9, 93–4; interactions with
others 84–5; language 93; learning
styles 93, 94; motor skills 36–7;
reading 5, 93; sensory differences 5, 94;
stress 48; testosterone 92–3
Gerhardt, S. 17, 84, 102
gestures 47, 52, 68
Glaser, D. 64

glials 22
glucose 20
glutamate receptors 20–1
Goddard, S. 17, 20, 35
Goethe, J.W. von 2
Goldberg, E. 15, 19
Goldschmied, E. 3, 82, 83
Good Childhood, A 101
Gopnik, A. et al. 68, 69
government policies 103–4
Green, H. et al. 49
Gregory, R.L. 9
Grille, R. 100–1
Gross, K. 107n2
Gur, R.C. 19

Hall, D. 103
Hall, S. 103
hand–eye coordination 60–1, 63
Harlow, H. 54
health and safety 105
Health-Led Parenting Programme 103
Healthy Lives, Brighter Futures 103
hearing 26, 31–3, 94, 96
hindbrain 10, 11
hippocampus 13
Hodges, D.A. 40, 42
Hodson, D. 101
Honing, H. et al. 41
hormones 46, 92–3
Horwood, J. 27, 52
Hosking, G. 101
HPA-axis 13
Hughes, B. 4
hypothalamus 13

Iacoboni, M. 50
identity 6, 59, 70, 95, 102–3
imagination 69–70, 88
imitation 50–3, 69–70, 96
imperative pointing 63
implicit memory 66
impulse control 15–16
independence 56, 61, 66, 67–8, 70, 84, 101,
105
Infant Directed Speech (IDS) *see* motherese
interactions and relationships 38–
55, 106; faces 46–50; gender
differences 84–5; imitation 50–3; lack of
communication 42–4, 60, 62, 104, 106;
motherese 32, 40–4, 47, 108n6; sensory
experiences 18, 26, 27; in the womb 39–
40; *see also* attachment; separation anxiety

Internet 89

Jaffe, J. et al. 44
Jarman, E. 30
Johnston, M.V. 20
joyfulness 81

Karr-Morse, R. 73, 81
key person approach 82–4, 95
Knickmeyer, R. et al. 20
Kugiumutzakis, G. et al. 50

Laming reports 80, 103
language 16, 33, 42–3, 67, 93; *see also*
    motherese
Larson, K. 108n6
Layard, R. 101, 103
learning disabilities 57
learning styles 93, 94
LeDoux, J. 9
Leslie, A. 75
Levin, F.M. 20
Lewis, T.L. et al. 11, 14, 49, 53, 54, 60, 79
Lieberman, A.E. et al. 85, 86
light sensitivity 30–1
Lillard, A. 75
limbic system *see* emotional brain
'little Neros' 70, 71–4
Llinas, R.R. 41
Locke, J.L. 23
loneliness 58, 65–6
long-term memory 66–7
long-term potentiation 21
Lorch, C.A. et al. 40
Lorenz, K. 54
loss and grief 85–7
Luria, A. 15

McClure, A. 36, 92, 93, 94
McElwain, N.L. 64
MacLean, P.D. 9
mammalian brain *see* emotional brain
Marano, H.E. 105
Meaney, M.J. et al. 18
Meltzoff, A.N. 50, 52, 66, 109n11
memory 13, 63, 66–7
mental disorders 49, 98–9
Messinger, D.S. 48
midbrain 10, 11
mind 9
mirror neurons 24, 50–3
mirror recognition 69, 88
mobility 67, 68

Moore, Mary Sue 3
Moore, M.K. 109n11
motherese 32, 40–4, 47, 108n6
mothers: with depression 39, 43, 48;
    well-being in pregnancy 39–40; *see also*
    adults: awareness and sensitivity; adults:
    emotional needs; attachment; interactions
    and relationships; motherese
motor functions 26, 94
motor skills 35–6
movement 26, 34–7, 41
muscle development 36–7, 63, 94
music 40, 41, 42, 46–7
myelination 22, 23

Nagy, E. 52
National Institute of Child Health and
    Human Development (NICHD) 64
National Literacy Trust 44
National Science Foundation 46
nature and nurture 9, 18
neglect 45–6, 50
Nelson, C.A. 23–4
'neural footprint' 8, 50, 53, 73, 78–9, 99
neural groove 10
neural networks 21, 36, 61, 65, 77
neural plate 10
neurons 20–2
neurotransmitters 21–2, 46
Newberger, E.H. 93–4
news stories 89
Next Generation, The 101
NICHD (National Institute of Child Health
    and Human Development) 64
nightmares 76, 88

Oberman, L.M. 51, 53
object permanence 63, 70
occipital lobe 14
O'Connor, T.G. et al. 40, 48
Olds, D. 103
O'Neill, M. et al. 52–3
opiods 46
orbital pre-frontal cortex 15, 71
orbitofrontal cortex 64–5
over-sensitive stress response system 58–9
overprotection 105
Oxfordshire County Council Sure Start
    95–6
oxytocin 46

Palmer, S. 102
Panksepp, J. 26, 46, 62, 73, 75

parentese *see* motherese
parents *see* adults: awareness and sensitivity;
    adults: emotional needs; attachment;
    interactions and relationships; motherese;
    mothers
parietal love 14
Patrick, W. 46, 101
pattern 41
peer relationships 77
Perry, B. 14, 15, 50, 57
personal, social and health education 103
Phillips, D.A. 102
Piaget, J. 50
pituitary gland 13
play 36, 69, 74–6, 77, 87–8, 105, 107n2;
    absence of play 75–6
pointing 63–4
posture 32–3, 35–6, 51
pre-frontal cortex 15
Preger, J. 102
pregnancy: well-being of mother 39–40
pretence 69, 75
Primary National Literacy Strategy 44
Primary National Strategy 103
Prinz, W. 50
Prior, V. 64
procedural memory 66–7
professional bias 90–1
proprioceptive sense 26

Quartz, S. 11

Ramachandran, V.S. 30, 51, 53
reaching and grasping 30, 36, 51, 60–1
Read, V. 83
reading 5, 44, 93, 94, 105
Reddy, V. 16, 24, 60
reflexes 35
refugees 86
relationships *see* interactions and
    relationships
reptilian brain *see* brain stem
responsibility 80–1
reward 62–3
rhythm 41
Rizolatti, G. et al. 50
Robinson, M. 33
role play 69, 74, 75, 76, 77

Sachs, O. 41
Sax, L. 94
Schiffman, H.R. 32, 34
Schofield, G. 54

Schonkoff, J.P. 102
school 83–4
Schore, A. 15, 17, 24, 65
'seeking' system 62
Sejnowski, T.J. 11
self-awareness 2, 68, 69–70, 71
self-esteem 81
self-harm 62–3
self-regulation 64–5, 72, 77
self-reliance 84
semantic memory 67
sense of self 6, 70, 95, 102–3
senses 8, 24–37; development 25–6; and
    gender 5, 94; hearing 26, 31–3, 94, 96;
    movement 26, 34–7, 41; smell 26, 33–4;
    synesthesia 25; taste 26, 33–4; touch 18,
    27–9; vision 26, 29–31
separation and divorce 85–6, 101
separation anxiety 45–6, 60, 61, 64, 84–5, 87
sharing 12, 77
Sheets-Johnstone, M. 34–5
short-term memory 13
siblings 76, 86–7
Siegel, D.J. 9, 15, 18–19
singing 42, 44
sleep 61
'Smartie experiment' 109–10n11
smell 26, 33–4
social referencing 63–4
society 106
Sparrow, J.D. 68
St. Clair, C. et al. 18
startle reflex 11
Stein, J.F. 20
step-families 86–7
'sticky fixation' 29, 48, 52
'still face' experiment 43, 48–9, 52, 85
Stokes, G. 98
Stoodley, C.J. 20
'strange situation' 55, 90
stranger anxiety 64–5, 68
Strathearn, L. et al. 48
stress: antenatal stress 40; and the brain 13;
    child's reactions to 48, 58–9, 67
subcortical brain *see* emotional brain
Sunderland, M. 23, 45, 46, 58, 70, 102
Sure Start Children's Centres 103
symbolic representation 75
synapses 21, 22–3
synesthesia 25

Talge, N. et al. 40
taste 26, 33–4

television 28, 43, 62, 65, 89, 104
temper tantrums 68, 70–4, 77
temperament 72–5, 82
temperature 27
temporal lobe 14
territoriality 11–12
testosterone 92–3
thalamus 13
theory of mind 75, 109–10n11
Think Family 103
threats 12, 13, 64, 87–9
toilet training 87, 88
touch 18, 27–9
traveller children 86
Trevarthen, C. 16, 17, 24, 39, 41, 42, 43,
    56, 57
Tronick, E. 43, 48
turn taking 77

unconscious memory 66
UNICEF 101
Unique Child 37, 38

values 6
vestibular sense 26, 32–3
vision 26, 29–31
voice 105

Walsh, I. 101
Watson, J. 101
WAVE report 101
weaning 33, 61
Wiley, M.S. 73, 81
Wolf, M. 4
working memory 66, 67

Zeedyk, S. 44, 51, 52, 76, 104